Cindy McDowell creatively weaves stories and quilt patterns into an insightful, hopeful look at life that both encourages and inspires the reader, splashing light on her world in the process—I highly recommend *Quilts From Heaven.*

CHERI FULLER, AUTHOR OF
Extraordinary Kids!

Cindy is an extraordinary woman who has led no ordinary life. How grateful I am that she has stitched so many of her life-lessons together in this beautiful volume! If you've ever wondered how all the pieces of your life fit together, this book is for you.

MAGGIE WALLEM ROWE, DIRECTOR OF
Women's Ministries for
Vision New England

Cindy graces our weary spiritual shoulders with a warm, personalized quilt of perspective, filling it with the comforting loft of her own deep lessons in trust and hope. After reading her book, I'll never look at another quilt without thinking how it symbolizes God's perfect plan for the scraps of our lives.

JEANNE ZORNES, AUTHOR OF
When I Got on the Highway to Heaven
. . . I Didn't Expect Rocky Roads

Quilts From Heaven is a powerful and unique way to encourage faith in our great God who can take the scraps of our lives and piece together a marvelous work that glorifies him. Cindy has increased my trust in God through her inspirational stories woven from the beautiful example of quilts. Her words made me want to create my own quilt and meditate on God's goodness in my life.

KATHY COLLARD MILLER, AUTHOR OF
God's Abundance

Cindy meticulously brings to life the timeless art of patchwork quilting . . . all the while stitching together a rich treasury of unchanging truths.

SHARON ANDERSON, AUTHOR OF
And the Two Became One Plus

Every quilt has a story. In *Quilts From Heaven* the stories are spiritual ones. Using quilts as examples, Cindy shows how God has pieced knowledge, pain, and growth on life's road to create the heirloom quilt that is her life thus far. Moving illustrations and insightful instruction bind together to form a delightful volume that warms the heart.

EILEEN WESTFALL, AUTHOR OF
Quilts Say It Best

In *Quilts From Heaven* Cindy weaves a seamless partnership of fabric and faith. Her spiritual insights are relevant and deep; her move from needle to heart is so natural that I (who would rather do anything than sew) found the reading both profitable and pleasurable. Cindy McDowell's *Quilt* may not be an heirloom, but it is, in my opinion, a genuine treasure! I commend it to you. Treat yourself and then pass the blessing on to someone you love.

COLLEEN TOWNSEND EVANS, AUTHOR OF
The Vine Life

I felt deeply encouraged by *Quilts From Heaven.* Cindy's words settle in comforting folds around my heart and remind me that God is near. His love envelops me like these quilts and promises to make today's broken pieces in my life a thing of service and beauty for someone tomorrow. I needed that.

VIRELLE KIDDER, AUTHOR OF
Loving, Launching, and Letting Go

Inspiring, encouraging, affirming! Skillfully woven bits of humor, words of wisdom, and poignant sketches of courageous pioneer women—all this you will find in this marvelous new book by Cindy McDowell. *Quilts From Heaven* is satisfying reading in the deepest sense of the word. The connection between family life and a quilt, between spiritual insight and down-home neighborliness shines through its pages.

INGRID TROBISCH, AUTHOR OF
Keeper of the Springs

Appealing to our artistic nature, Cindy's quilt weaves patterns that will challenge, comfort, and encourage you in your own faith journey.

SUSAN A. YATES, AUTHOR OF
A House Full of Friends

You'll have a hard time putting this book down once you have started reading! Let God speak to you about your own "patchwork of life" and how it, too, can become a parable in someone else's life.

CHRIS ADAMS,
Women's Enrichment,
LifeWay Christian Resources

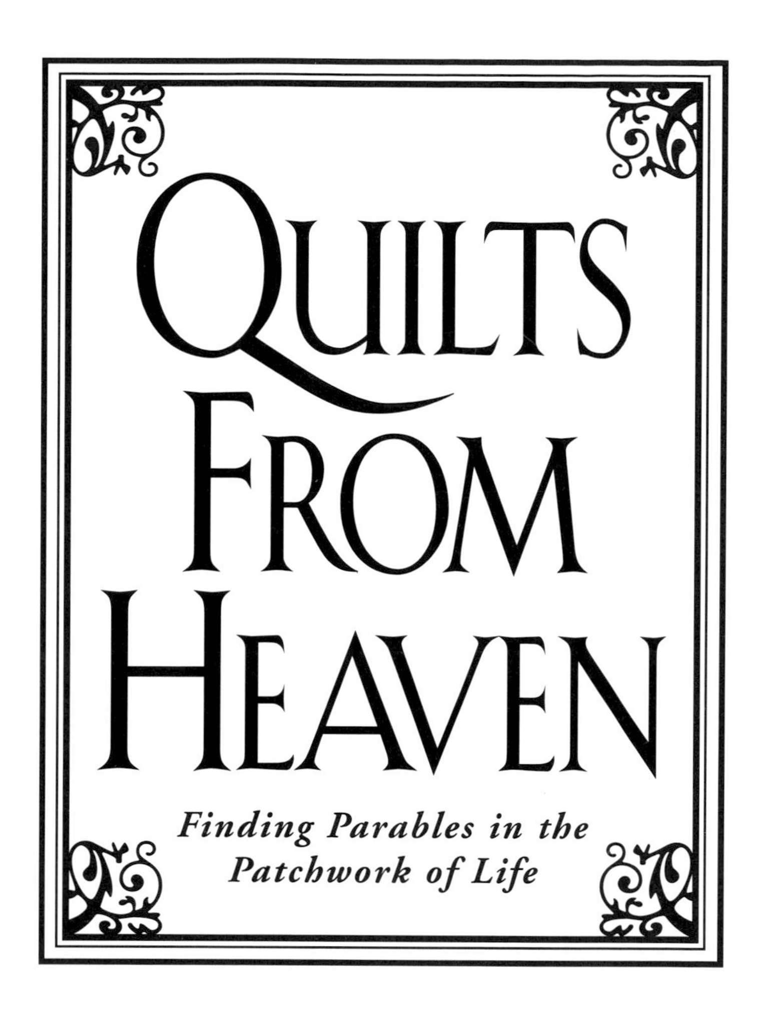

Quilts From Heaven

Finding Parables in the Patchwork of Life

Lucinda Secrest McDowell

Broadman & Holman Publishers

Nashville, Tennessee

0-8054-1099-6

Published by Broadman & Holman Publishers, Nashville, Tennessee
Editorial Team: Vicki Crumpton, Janis Whipple, Kim Overcash
Interior Design and Photography Art Direction:
Paul T. Gant Design, Nashville, Tennessee
Interior and Cover Photography, except for Job's Tears:
G. W. Austin Photography, Nashville, Tennessee.

Photograph of Job's Tears: Myron Miller Photography,
New York, New York.
Typesetting: Desktop Miracles, Dallas, Texas

Dewey Decimal Classification: 242
Subject Heading: CHRISTIAN WOMEN—RELIGIOUS LIFE /
QUILTS—MISCELLANEA
Library of Congress Card Catalog Number: 98-31315

Library of Congress Cataloging-in-Publication Data

McDowell, Lucinda Secrest, 1953–
Quilts from heaven : finding parables in the patchwork of life / Lucinda Secrest McDowell.
p. cm.
ISBN 0-8054-1099-6
1. Christian women—Religious life. 2. Patchwork quilts—Miscellanea. I. Title.
BV4527.M39 1999
242'.643—dc21

98-31315
CIP

1 2 3 4 5 03 02 01 00 99

For My Parents
Nathaniel Pratt Secrest
and
Sarah Hasty Secrest

With Love and Gratitude on
Your Fiftieth Wedding Anniversary!

Thanks for starting my quilt
forty-five years ago!

TABLE OF CONTENTS

ACKNOWLEDGMENTS

My life has been shaped and influenced by many people. So has this book! I'm grateful to all who participated in the "quilting bee" it took to make all the pieces become a whole. A special thanks to . . .

- My husband and life partner, Mike, for so much . . . but especially his shouldering the many extra family and home responsibilities while I was writing.
- My children—Justin, Tim, Fiona, and Maggie Sarah—who will always be my greatest inspiration for living out my legacy each day with grace and hope. I love you to pieces!
- My best friend and daily encourager, Maggie Rowe, whose New Year's resolution was to pray ten minutes each day for God to anoint my writing.
- "Heartspring," my circle of prayer and support who helped keep me focused on my passion of communicating God's faithfulness and grace—Cynthia Fantasia, Diane Averill, Helen Boursier, Sharon Anderson, Karen Hearl, Linda Anderson, Lynne Rienstra, Jean Marrapodi, Margaret Barton, Sharon Dietrich, and Maggie Rowe.
- Special quilters who readily shared their knowledge and resources—Aileen McDonough, Paula Vining,

Debbie McKinnis, Sarah Secrest, and Kathi Johnson.

- "Daybreak," my weekly early morning prayer group who always provided coffee and comfort—Karen Memmott, Jessica Parchman, Kathi Johnson, Judy Franzen, and Aileen McDonough.

- Computer experts who continue to usher me into the fascinating and challenging world of high technology—Jane Benard, Jean Marrapodi, and David Luce.

- Friends who provided meals, housecleaning, child care, and even a chalet in Quebec during my "writing crunch" time—Faith, Mike and Maggie, Ed and Kay, Cindy, Linda, Aileen, Karen, Liz, and Susan.

- Other authors who encouraged me in this project—Carol Kent, Elisabeth Elliot, Gail MacDonald, Jeanne Zornes, Robin Gunn, Karen Mains, Coke Evans, Virelle Kidder, Sharon Anderson, and Ingrid Trobisch.

- My editor, Vicki Crumpton, for believing I could weave fabric and faith into stories someone might read, and my project editor, Janis Whipple, for making a beautiful pattern from the many pieces of this book.

- My church family and staff colleagues at the place "where the Spirit is alive and miracles happen"—First Church of Christ Congregational in Old Wethersfield, Connecticut.

- My parents, Pratt and Sarah Secrest, for daily prayers and funny phone calls to keep me going. And my sisters—Cathy Secrest Ray and Susan Secrest Waters—for being friends and prayer partners as well as sisters.

- Jesus Christ, who knows all about broken pieces and who promises to make something beautiful from the scraps of my life.

PIECES OF MY QUILT

If quilts could *talk*
I'd like to think I'd hear just what they'd say,
"I'll hold you close within my folds and wipe your tears away.
I'll keep you warm and give you strength to face another day."
If quilts could talk . . .

If quilts could *sing*
I'd like to think I'd recognize each tune,
The lullaby or funeral dirge or wedding march in June.
Both sweet and haunting melodies I'd listen to them croon.
If quilts could sing . . .

If quilts could *write*
I'd like to think I'd read the words they'd pen,
Of life and love and motherhood, of mystery without end.
And, oh, the drama they could share of everywhere they'd been.
If quilts could write . . .

If quilts could *pray,*
I'd like to think I'd feel each heartfelt prayer
Of thankfulness or great concern for those within their care;
Petitions to a loving God—the One who's always there.
If quilts could pray . . .

The quilt of my own life
Finds voice to *talk, sing, write,* and *pray,*
As it weaves a hundred stories in its own eclectic way.
And with each stitch of grace and hope my legacy is built;
All fragments finally made a whole . . .
the *pieces of my quilt.*

LUCINDA SECREST McDOWELL

Practice
Makes
Perfect
slw
1984

CHAPTER ONE

SAMPLER

I pushed back my long hair, made stringy by the humidity of the Kentucky summer day. I was wearing only cutoff overalls, a T-shirt, and flip-flops, but I was still hot. I glanced around the circle as my needle moved in and out of the heavy material that was locked into the frame suspended from the ceiling. Both Alice and Jewell seemed cool and comfortable handling the winter cover on this summer day. Of course, they already had a lifetime of quilting under their belts. For me, this was only the beginning. . . .

It has been twenty-five years since I made my first quilt.

That summer I turned twenty and announced to my horrified parents that I would be working as a missionary in the poverty-stricken mining area of Kentucky. I lived up in that "holler" with a seventy-five-year-old quilter named Alice Dean. She took me along with her to collect the scraps of material that the coat factory tossed out each day. She taught me how to sew the pieces together to make a pretty patterned top. Finally, she showed me how to join the top, the flannel backing, and the stuffing with stitches.

We quilted on an old frame that hung from the ceiling in the church house adjoining her property. During the day I supervised recreational programs for the "holler" kids and shared the love of Jesus. At night I pieced quilts with Mrs. Dean and washed my hair in rainwater because electricity and running water hadn't reached that "holler" yet.

In the intervening years since, every one of my own children has slept under one of Mrs. Dean's quilts. And tonight when I tucked in my youngest for what looked to be the night of a great ice storm, I covered her as I do each night with that very first quilt I made twenty-five years ago in that old church house in Kentucky.

I've made other quilts since then, but I'm still no great quilter. I just happen to love them. I believe a project that takes li'l ole bits of leftover pieces of material and transforms them into works of art that not only comfort, but inspire, can't be half bad.

The word *quilt* is derived from the Latin *culcita,* which literally means "a stuffed sack." A true quilt must be composed of three parts: a top, a batting (lining), and a backing. Some people refer to them as "textile sandwiches," which I believe is as good a definition as any. Not only is *quilt* a noun, but it is also a verb. The actual *quilting* is the process of stitching to hold the three layers together and prevent the filling from shifting.

The quilt top is the decorative layer and is often made by piecing or patchwork. Here's where the creativity takes shape—individual cutting, organizing, placing, and stitching of many pieces of fabric together. "To appreciate the precision of working with tiny sections, consider that if the measurement of just one edge of one piece is not perfectly aligned, the plan of the entire quilt top can be jeopardized."[1]

I think it was the pioneer women in America whose needles helped create a way of life that influenced a whole cultural and social structure:

> No other art was so completely dominated by women or brought so many together to work, including young ladies, for in the eighteenth century they were rigorously taught that usefulness was happiness. And there was no better way to make oneself useful than to sew.
>
> As early as age four, little girls began practicing their stitches. Holding a delicate needle in their tiny, clumsy fingers, they pieced together simple four-patch blocks of plain and flowered calicoes. One woman described her childhood experience, "Before I was three years old, I was started at piecing a quilt. Patchwork, you know. My stint was at first only two blocks a day, but these were sewn together with the

greatest of care or they were unraveled and done over." By the time young women were about to be married, the needle had become their constant companion, and they took great pride in the accomplished needlework of their quilts.[2]

Traditionally, twelve quilt tops were to be finished before a girl's engagement. She was never to start her thirteenth quilt until after her betrothal was officially announced. Then her bridal quilt was planned and executed, usually by close friends and family of the bride.

Caroline Cowles Richards noted in her diary in 1862: "I have been up at Laura Chapin's from 10 o'clock in the morning until 10 at night, finishing Jennie Howell's bed quilt, as she is to be married very soon. Almost all of the girls were there. We finished it at 8 p.m.; and when we took it off the frames, we gave three cheers!"

When I see old quilts, I feel a sense of pride in the stalwart women who made them. Back in the eighteenth century, quilts were one of the few household items over which women had full control, since everything else belonged to their husbands. Ruth Finley, in *Old Patchwork Quilts and the Women Who Made Them,* states that "women with little or no knowledge of mathematics were capable of planning and piecing the most intricate geometric designs, transforming scraps of fabric into breathtaking harmonies of color and design to add beauty to their surroundings."[3]

Most of all, they put their lives into their quilts. This is quite evident in the writings of Margaret Ickis's great-grandmother, an Ohio quilter:

> It took me more than twenty years, nearly twenty-five, I reckon, in the evening after supper when the children were all put to bed. My whole life is in that quilt. It scares me sometimes when I look at it. All my joys and all my sorrows are stitched into those little pieces. When I was right proud of the boys and when I was downright provoked and angry with them. When the girls annoyed me or when they gave me a warm feeling around my heart. And John too. He was stitched into that quilt and all the thirty years we were married. Sometimes I loved him and sometimes I sat there hating him as I pieced the patches together. So they are all in that quilt, my hopes and fears, my joys and sorrows, my loves and hates. I tremble sometimes when I remember what that quilt knows about me.[4]

My own life is a lot like the Sampler quilt. Each block is different and represents a different story, a different pattern. Samplers were usually made by young girls as a teaching project. By making their mistakes in the various blocks on their Sampler, they were able to learn and then go on—perhaps to do an entire quilt in that block they had just mastered.

If my life is like a quilt, then surely God is the Divine Quilter. How lovingly he gathers up the scraps and remnants and leftovers of my experiences, my brokenness, and my joy. With the skillful needlework of grace, he stitches it all together to make a wonderful whole.

Nothing is wasted. In the Quilter's hand, all that I perceived as useless rags—all those times I blew it and

disappointed God and others I love—are part of the perfect patchwork pattern he has planned just for me. All the various colors, textures, and shapes will somehow come together to accomplish something beautiful. Even his stitching covers over my mistakes. Truly I can say with an elderly King Solomon as he reflected on his life: "[God] hath made every thing beautiful in his time" (Eccles. 3:11 KJV).

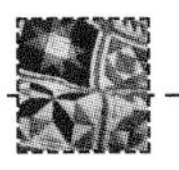

If my life is like a quilt,
then surely God is the Divine Quilter.
How lovingly he gathers up the scraps and
remnants and leftovers of my experiences,
my brokenness, and my joy.
With the skillful needlework of grace,
he stitches it all together to make
a wonderful whole.

One prairie woman in 1870 wrote, "I make them warm to keep my family from freezing; I make them beautiful to keep my heart from breaking."

Do you sometimes feel as though your life is in pieces? I often feel that way as I pray, "Lord, gather me together." Then my eye catches sight of the heart-shaped patchwork plaque on my wall that reads: "When Life gives you scraps, make quilts!" So I collect the leftovers and offer them to God.

One of my sewing friends likens the fabric remnants to the lives many people offer to the Lord at salvation: "The best part gone, the years wasted, they come to him holding only strips and odd pieces. But that doesn't stop the Master Designer. He knows a pattern exactly right for each person. Deftly, kindly, he cuts out the form, joins the raw seams and fashions what was nearly discarded into something desirable."[5]

My soul rejoices in my God.
For he has clothed me with garments of salvation
and arrayed me in a robe of righteousness. (Isa. 61:10)

Just as Sampler quilts were the beginning point for most young seamstresses, so my Sampler prompts me to answer the question: "Why write a book on quilting at this time—the dawn of the new millennium?" Perhaps it's because I want to recapture something that has been lost in the fuss and fury of my life as a modern woman. For me, the quilt is a symbol.

I see parables—stories—in the quilts: Back to when people had time to tell stories and to hear them. For some, the quilt was (and is) a "testimony to a time when pressures did not cry out for urgent things to be constantly tended to, when the world had not created a thousand different temptations pulling free time into a myriad of mindless

activities. It told of values and patience and timeless meanings. It drew the person in. It spoke of comfort and rest. It soothed with the gentleness of a mother's kiss."[6]

Women seek this. We need it. One quilter in Bakersfield, California, was interviewed recently for a newspaper article. She's part of a quilter's group called "The Material Girls." Her response to the interviewer's question "Why quilting?" was this: "When you quilt, you tie into all the other quilts done by women. . . . It makes you gentle, softens the blows the real world gives us. If you feel unloved, dumb, and stupid, just curl up in a chair and quilt."[7]

But a book on quilts does more than bring back the nostalgic past—it also challenges us to look forward and examine what our own legacy will be. What are the stories of my life? Is it too late to change them? One reason I can face the unknown future of the new millennium is that, by taking time to reflect, I now better see God's weaving of fabric and faith thus far.

We all quilt for different reasons. "One woman quilts and begins to gather a sense of wholeness from the fragments of her life. Another quilts to help mend the world's brokenness. Still another woman takes up her needle to hand a legacy of warmth and love to her children—a legacy that will continue into the next generation and the next."[8] But one thing abides—when the project is finished, there is a whole where there once were only parts. This is tremendously satisfying to the quilter. And that's what I desire when the quilt of my life is finally complete: that my Maker will rejoice in the whole—and be satisfied.

Join me now on this journey of discovering parables in the patchwork of life. Learn about the patterns, and snuggle up in the comfort of knowing that all that happens in life has meaning when placed in the hands of the God who created us and loves us far more than we'll ever know.

CHAPTER TWO

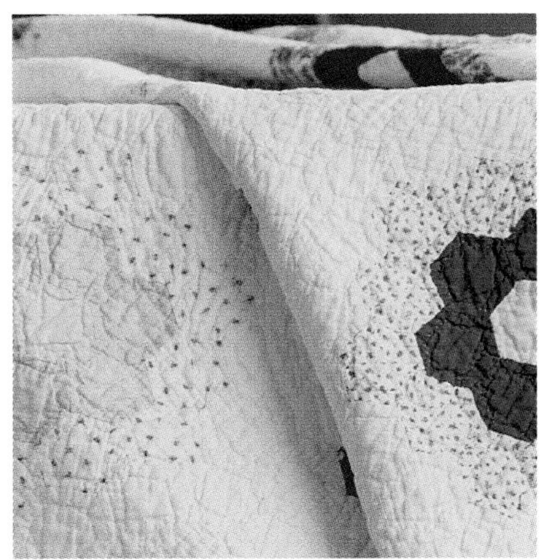

GRANDMOTHER'S FLOWER GARDEN

My mama was born with a green thumb. One of my daddy's favorite stories is about the time my older sister started to talk, and he wanted to show her off. He had trained her well and started off by asking, "Cathy, what does the dog say?"

"Woof, woof," came her answer, right on cue.

"And what does the cow say?" he prodded.

"Moo, moo," she beamed in response.

"Cathy, what does your mama say?" Daddy grinned.

"Buy more pot plants!" Cathy shrieked with laughter.

My mama didn't think it was that funny at the time, but we all get a kick out of the story today. However, I sometimes

have to explain that my genteel Southern mama didn't grow marijuana in the fifties. *Pot plants* was simply our vernacular for potted plants. In other words, she loved to garden.

She still does.

I wish I could say that it rubbed off on me. It didn't. I am what is known in politically correct circles as *horticulturally challenged.* Houseplants take one look at me and wither. It's sad to be a flower lover and a flower killer at the same time.

Thankfully, no green thumb is needed in quilting. Grandmother's Flower Garden is a beautiful quilt pattern made of circular arrangements of hexagonal flowers. Usually, many tiny scrap pieces are used—the more variety of fabric, the more beautiful the overall picture of the quilt.

God has chosen to teach me about life through my efforts in the gardening field. Back in 1970 I adopted Isaiah 58:10–11 as my "life verse," a promise from God to hold before me throughout my life. Almost thirty years later I can see how utterly prophetic it has been:

If you spend yourselves in behalf of the hungry
and satisfy the needs of the oppressed,
then your light will rise in the darkness,
and your night will become like the noonday.
The Lord will guide you always;
he will satisfy your needs in a sun-scorched land
and will strengthen your frame.
You will be like a well-watered garden,
like a spring whose waters never fail.

Gardens are a lot like quilts in that they recycle leftovers. Just as a quilter starts by gathering lots of scraps and pieces, the gardener gets the soil ready by mixing up dirt with decaying living organisms. This makes humus—a very rich soil, perfect for growth. The dead stuff actually helps other stuff live! Jesus talked a lot about dying to our old nature. (The word *humility* comes from the root word *humus.*) That decaying old nature mixes with our souls and creates a spiritual soil that is very fertile, producing a rich crop of spiritual fruit.

All of us want the fruit, the blossoms, the results. But how many of us are willing to be buried under dirt and mud for a time? Yet, that's exactly what happens to bulbs. They spend all winter under the frozen ground, and it doesn't appear that anything is happening. But just because we can't see the bulb doesn't mean it isn't growing. Eventually, little shoots poke up through the ground, and then the daffodils, crocuses, and hyacinths appear. So there was some activity going on after all!

Is your bulb buried deep in the earth right now? Is it the winter season for you? Are you at a time in your life when you cannot see any good? Are you dying?

Christina Rossetti felt that way back in the nineteenth century and shared her feelings in the following portion of her poem, "A Better Resurrection":

My life is like a faded leaf,
My harvest dwindled to a husk;
Truly my life is void and brief
And tedious in the barren dusk;

My life is like a frozen thing,
No bud nor greenness can I see:
Yet rise it shall—the Sap of spring;
O Jesus, rise in me.[1]

My friend Jessica gave me a bookmark that makes a lot of sense. It says: "If you pray for rain, be prepared for a little mud!" There's nothing wrong with praying for rain—as long as we remember that the Bible says it rains on both the just and the unjust.

The same rain that provides water to sustain life also stirs up quite a bit of mud. Hurricanes leave a lot of mud and destruction in their wake. Floods devastate towns and countrysides. Tidal waves can wipe out villages, even entire islands. Yet if water is such a force to be reckoned with, why do you suppose God makes it so clear that we can't live without it? Because nothing worthwhile ever came easy.

Jesus said, "Very truly, I tell you, unless a grain of wheat falls into the earth and dies, it remains just a single grain; but if it dies, it bears much fruit" (John 12:24 NRSV). If we want fruit (or blossoms), then we must be willing to be buried under dirt and mud, even to the point of death.

But some dying leads to life, and some leads to only death. We all suffer. We all get stuck in the mud when the rains come. Some of us even know that this is necessary for our growth. But what makes the difference in the outcome? Could it be the roots? Scientists say the taller a tree is, the deeper its roots must go in order to sustain it from destructive winds and rain.

And what about drought? To keep from withering, a tree must send roots down into the constantly moist depths of the

earth—the mud. And if we are to weather life's dry times, our delight in God's Word must be a continual process. An occasional soaking won't do. In Scripture we read:

> *Blessed is the man who trusts in the Lord,*
> *whose confidence is in him.*
> *He will be like a tree planted by the water*
> *that sends out its roots by the stream.*
> *It does not fear when heat comes;*
> *its leaves are always green.*
> *It has no worries in a year of drought*
> *and never fails to bear fruit.*
> *(Jer. 17:7–8)*

Gardeners must also deal with weeds. I assume there are no weeds in Grandmother's Flower Garden quilts. There are, however, plenty of weeds in Grandmother's and everyone else's gardens. Weeds are defined as "plants out of place." What to do with them? Pull them out by the roots! Clip and cut away anything that gets in the way of the fruit and blossoms we so desperately want for harvest.

Jesus portrays a loving God as the Good Gardener who cuts and trims anything that would impede our growth. "I am the true vine, and my Father is the gardener. He cuts away every branch of mine that doesn't produce fruit. But he trims clean every branch that does produce fruit, so that it will produce even more fruit" (John 15:1–3 CEV).

Cutting hurts, doesn't it. But it helps me to know that the original Greek word for *cut* in that verse was *airo. Airo*

has at least two meanings: one is "to cut off," but the other is "to lift up." Max Lucado, in his book *A Gentle Thunder*, points out that both meanings are implied here: "Before God cuts a fruitless branch, he lifts it up. A gardener does this. He repositions the fruitless branch so it can get more sun or more space. . . . A good vine dresser will stretch the vine on the arbor to afford it more air and sun."[2]

I've seen my mama realign a plant, and I've also seen God realign a life. Years ago, God quite unexpectedly (well, unexpected for us—he certainly wasn't taken by surprise) uprooted our family from the South and moved us into a ministry here in New England. At the time we felt cut off from our church, friends we loved, and our home. The circumstances of the sudden move took their toll on my spirit, and I suffered depression as a result of too many unwanted changes in my life. Yet it was during that very time that God clearly reached down and brought us into a whole new understanding of his grace. God breathed a new life into me—but he had to cut me off from everything comfortable and familiar first.

Yes, pruning hurts—especially pruning back. As I write these words God is forcing a friend of mine to prune back. She has had to cancel speaking engagements and say no to many good things. For awhile it may look a little bleak on the production side of the ledger. But the pruning is for a purpose, known only to God. My friend isn't sure of all God is up to in her life, but she does know that his purpose is to produce more and different fruit in her for the future. She relies on the following promise: "No discipline seems pleasant at the time, but painful. Later on, however, it produces

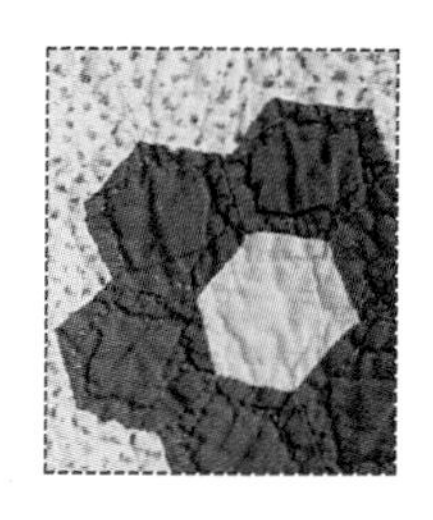

a harvest of righteousness and peace for those who have been trained by it" (Heb. 12:11).

I spent many years striving to please God, trying to make myself into a beautiful flower for his garden. But the more I tried and failed, the more defeated I became. Because my goal was to earn God's love, God's favor, and God's power, I was missing the whole point of the Christian life. My seed was buried all right, but my death wasn't leading to new life.

With each new defeat another limb was cut off, until one day I faced God as nothing but a bunch of old stubs and roots—not a flower, not even a fruit-bearing plant. I was at the end of myself. And that was exactly where God wanted me to be.

The Master Gardener said, "Cindy, I want to teach you about grace—a gift you don't deserve and can never earn, but grace is the very gift I bestow on you that will allow you to blossom in my way and in my timing."

I had read about the fruit of the Spirit—"love, joy, peace, patience, kindness, goodness, faithfulness, gentleness and self-control" (Gal. 5:22–23)—and that was what I was seeking after. But what I really needed to do was to seek Christ, and then the fruit—the harvest—would be the by-product of a life lived in him.

Grandmother's Flower Garden is a beautiful picture of hexagonal blossoms, the fruit of someone's love and toil and skill with every stitch of hope and faithfulness. It is also the pattern the protagonist in T. Davis Bunn's novel *The Quilt* chooses to make at the end of her life. Mary decides that her last good work will be to bring the women of the community together in one last quilt-making project.

But when sick and elderly Mary announces she will make another quilt, everyone is shocked and reminds her that she's not up to it. All the women who have come to her for advice through the years then offer to help (which was Mary's sly plan all along). With very little experience in quilting, and yet eager to please this godly matriarch, each woman listens in silence to Mary's instructions: "'It came to me this morning as I was putting these things in the wash. For every stitch that goes into this quilt, I want you to say a prayer. And it can't be just any prayer. It has to be a prayer of thanksgiving.'"[3]

Pretty soon the making of this Grandmother's Flower Garden quilt literally transforms the town and all the people in it. At the same time, they are eager to finish it as they see Mary's health rapidly declining. She, however, is not hurried because she knows that gardens take time. "Every few minutes, Mary would remind them of their purpose, their responsibility to say a prayer of thanks with each stitch sewn. 'It doesn't matter if this quilt takes another twenty years,' Mary would say a dozen times a day. 'What is important is that we all, each and every one of us, remember what it's like to be grateful.'"[4]

When the quilt is finally finished, it contains a sky blue sashing between each hexagonal flower consisting of fourteen petals made from different materials. "Somehow the different colors and designs and prints melted together and formed a new, larger pattern. The older ladies who had done quilts before knew this was the key. If the patterns were in true harmony they were seen yet not seen, like each brush stroke of a painting was not seen separately from the whole."[5]

We will not see the final harvest of our lives perhaps until eternity. But if the God who makes things grow (1 Cor. 3:7) has stitched Grandmother's Flower Garden into the quilt of this horticulturally challenged daughter of his, think of all he can do for you!

"If you sow to your own flesh, you will reap corruption from the flesh; but if you sow to the Spirit, you will reap eternal life from the Spirit. So let us not grow weary in doing what is right, for we will reap at harvest-time, if we do not give up" (Gal. 6:8–9 NRSV).

SUSAN SECREST

CHAPTER THREE

FRIENDSHIP QUILT

"Make new friends, but keep the old, one is silver and the other gold. A ring is round, it has no end, that's how long I want to be your friend," sang the Brownie Scouts gathered in a circle around me. I sang, too, and then we closed the meeting with the traditional daisy chain hand squeeze.

Watching the excited seven-year-olds scatter about to gather their things, I thought back almost forty years to when I, too, had been a Brownie instead of a Scout mom. Things were not so different. We had met in a Methodist church in a small Southern town. My daughter Maggie's troop meets in her school in a small New England town.

Yet both Maggie and I still sing the same song about friendship. I look at her as we leave and wonder what her life of friendships will be like. I then look back at the many who have been pieced into the Friendship Quilt of my own life.

Friendship Quilts began as a fad in the early 1840s along the New England seacoast, where every woman seemed to be making them. The patterns were the same simple ones used for other scrap quilts made at that time, and they were inexpensive since all that was required were remnant pieces of clothing.

Part of the fun, as well as the uniqueness, of the Friendship Quilt was that the girls and women made squares, put their names or short verses on them, and then swapped with their friends. After collecting enough squares from all around, the pieces were sewn together with sashing and finally stitched together. The result? A unique memory album of those one really cared about.

Friendship Quilts were especially popular as farewell gifts when families moved West. The men generally made the decision to move West (usually without consulting their wives and daughters, I might add). When the women packed up for their journey into the unknown, they said good-bye to all their friends and family, quite probably never to see them again. Friendship, or Album, Quilts containing the names and addresses of the womenfolk left behind helped provide an emotional link with those loved ones.

"For these reasons, the friendship quilt was steadily moving west over the Appalachians and Alleghenies, over the Wilderness Road and the National Road, into states such as Ohio and Michigan, Wisconsin and Kansas, by wagon, stage,

train, canal boat and steamboat. And, although patterns, fabrics and inked inscriptions varied from one region to another, America's friendship quilts are remarkably similar to each other."[1]

An article in the April 1888 issue of *Good Housekeeping* gave this advice: "Every young girl should piece one quilt at least to carry away with her to her husband's home, and if her lot happens to be cast among strangers, as is often the case, the quilt when she unfolds it will seem like the face of a familiar friend, and will bring up a whole host of memories, of mother, sister, friend, too sacred for us to intrude upon."[2]

Besides names, the quilt maker might choose to include other information, such as the town or township, county, state, or date. Especially on Friendship Quilts of the 1840s and 1850s, loving messages and verses—either biblical or secular—were written by the different quilt-block signers. Onto the Friendship Quilt made for New Jersey circuit rider David D. Graves in 1842, Elsworth Holeman penned, "How beautiful are the feet of them that preach the gospel of peace and bring glad tidings of good things."[3]

Betsey M. Wright of North Woodstock, Connecticut, received one block from a friend with these words:

Accept my friend this little pledge
Your love and friendship to engage
If e're we should be called to part
Let this be settled in your heart
That when this little piece you see
You ever will remember me.

M. E. A., WOODSTOCK, 1847[4]

I am reminded of the way my generation used to write sentiments in our school yearbooks, or the little autograph books I had at camp as a child. Back in the 1960s I also kept elaborate scrapbooks with clippings, photos, and cutouts from magazines. I'm delighted that there is now a revival of keeping memories and friendship albums. In fact, "memory books" are becoming big business if the large section in craft stores is any indication.

Whatever the medium, I believe it is important to take time to remember special friendships and to hold them in our hearts. My favorite definition of friendship is from the book *Friends and Friendship*: "A friend: a trusted confidant to whom I am mutually drawn as a companion and an ally, whose love for me is not dependent on my performance, and whose influence draws me closer to God."[5]

Sound good? When I share this definition with women, the next question they usually ask is: Where can I find that kind of friend? Now, that's a hard question to answer because friends pop up in the most unexpected places. I met one of my dearest friends, Janet, at a baseball game in Candlestick Park. We talked during the entire game. Afterwards her brother remarked, "I don't know why you talked to that girl the whole time. You'll probably never see her again."

Well, her brother may have a Ph.D. in higher mathematics, but he was dead wrong. Something clicked that day, and Janet and I spent the next several years traveling together, sharing our dreams, being in each other's weddings, and talking about motherhood and marriage to pastors.

There is no foolproof formula for making friends; however, there are some important guidelines. For instance, be the kind

of friend you want to have. A recent survey in *Today's Christian Woman* magazine discovered that 90 percent of women mark *trustworthiness* as the most important character trait they look for in a friend. As one observer of the survey said, "My friends don't care if I'm successful or have a good sense of humor. They just want to be able to trust me. In a world where change and transition are the norm, they want to know I'll be there for them."[6] The survey also discovered that a major reason for broken friendships was a betrayal of trust. So, what kind of friend are *you*? Can you be trusted?

Second to trustworthiness, 84 percent of the women surveyed counted *encouragement* as an important quality in a friendship. To *encourage* literally means to "give courage" to one another. What an important quality to develop when all around us hurting people long to be infused with hope and courage.

Perhaps encouragement—offering courage to the young women who were going away—was the most important value of the Friendship Quilts during the westward expansion of our country. "In carrying quilts, and especially friendship ones, on the overland trails, women could, in a sense, bring their loved ones with them. The staggering numbers of such quilts made during the height of the migrations to places like Ohio, Indiana, Illinois, Minnesota, Wisconsin, the Plains states, Oregon, and California in the 1840s and 1850s, and the care with which so many of them have been handed down, speak of their deeply felt value. They helped pioneers transcend the anguish and heal the pain of lifelong separations."[7]

And Friendship Quilts are flourishing again today! Quilting in America had quite a resurgence just before the

bicentennial celebration in 1976. That was also the year I made my first Friendship Quilt as a wedding gift to my younger sister, Susan.

Eight months before the wedding, I surreptitiously obtained names and addresses of special friends and family members of Susan and her fiancé, Glen. Along with a 10-inch square of muslin, I sent each person an invitation to participate in the making of the Wedding Quilt. They could use any colors and any style—patchwork, embroidery, appliqué, etc.—to create a square that represented their special relationship to the bride and groom. The only specific requirement was that somewhere on their square they were to place their name and a heart.

I eagerly checked my mailbox all during the fall of 1976. By the time winter set in at my cozy house in the Blue Ridge Mountains, I had fifty-six completed squares, so I began doing the quilting. Truly, love went into every stitch, for I not only loved my sister, but I also prayed for the marriage that would be built based on God's love.

The quilt was a wonderful surprise and success and was displayed at the wedding reception. Now, Susan and Glen, twenty-one years later, continue to live in the power of God's faithfulness and trusting his love. One day their quilt will be a precious legacy to pass on to their beautiful daughters.

I am grateful for the friends who have been woven into the Friendship Quilt of my own life. Each one is a unique treasure and has a special pattern of beauty. Perhaps the hardest aspect of friendship for me has been learning when expectations must be adjusted due to location, responsibilities, and the seasons of life. Even though it is unrealistic, I find it hard

to handle the changes that inevitably come as locations and situations change. I can relate to Melody Carlson, who had recently moved to a new town and was missing her old friends. She wrapped herself up in her grandmother's quilt and pondered:

> I thought of the many friends I'd had throughout my life. Some felt a bit scratchy and rough like a sturdy piece of wool, but in time they softened—or I became used to them. Others were delicate like silk and needed to be handled with care. Some were colorful and bright and great fun to be with. A few special others felt soft and cozy like flannel, and they knew how to make me feel better.
>
> Many of my friends have only been around for a season. So often I've had to leave them behind, or they leave me! And yet, in my heart, I know they are friends for life. . . . And that's because God has sewn them into my heart. I pulled the old quilt closer around me, comforted and warmed by memories. Surely, my own masterpiece—this quilt of friendships I fretted over—was not nearly finished, I would make new friends in this town.[8]

Like the friendship song says, I too will "make new friends" who will become threads of silver in my Friendship Quilt, but I will "keep the old," the threads of gold. And I will be thankful.

CHAPTER FOUR

SUNSHINE AND SHADOW

This morning trudging up the hill in the dark, I am glad I wore my snow boots. Even though it is technically spring, the New England terrain is still frozen with patches of ice. I grip my daughter's hand tightly and pull my heavy woolen coat around me, fully covering the bright Easter dress underneath.

We step carefully to avoid the tombstones, some dated as early as the seventeenth century. At the top of the hill, more than a hundred people are gathering to hear the Bible story of the first Easter. We haven't gathered in two days, since the service of Tenebrae, the gathering of shadows.

My husband and four children are all here. The teens vowed it would be the last time they agreed to wake up at 5:00 A.M. for this event. But since our youngest has never *not* observed Easter this way, she assumes that commemorating the empty tomb at the top of a cemetery hill at sunrise is "normal."

We are in the shadows, waiting for something. When it comes, it takes my breath away as I watch the sunshine creep up and cover God's creation as far as the eye can see. Our brass ensemble begins playing "Jesus Christ Is Risen Today," and we sing with gusto and hope.

Then, walking down to the church for our traditional sunrise breakfast, I sense that, somehow, the shadowy world has been infused with more than simply sunlight. The "Son Light" is being reflected in everyone I see, at least the folks who were up on the hill with me. We had been in the dark together, encountering obstacles along the way, claiming promises from God's Word, and waiting—always waiting—for the re-creation of a new day that we had been promised would come.

And it did come! Or, more precisely, *he* came. Perhaps the light seemed brighter because of the strong contrast to the darkness that preceded it. I suspect these feelings were not unlike what some of Christ's followers (and certainly the women at the tomb) felt so long ago. Of course, they had seen their whole world shattered with the supposed annihilation of their leader, the Messiah. They had witnessed his death. It had happened. But still they came. Those women still trudged to the tomb site in the darkness, before it was day. And when they left, it was most certainly light.

How quickly the joy followed the deep sorrow and despair! As Moltmann said, "God weeps with us so that we may someday laugh with Him."[1] Surely those early Christians must have felt as if their emotions were on a roller-coaster ride—down one moment and up the next. "Once all darkness, now as Christians you are light" (Eph. 5:8 NEB).

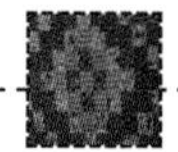

We had been in the dark together,
encountering obstacles along the way,
claiming promises from God's Word,
and waiting—always waiting—
for the re-creation of a new day
that we had been promised would come.

And it did come! Or, more precisely,
he came. Perhaps the light seemed brighter
because of the strong contrast to the
darkness that preceded it.

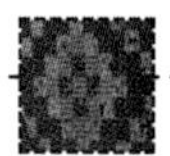

Life is full of contrasts, and I'm learning to embrace them, even when I hardly have time to breathe in between. It

was the wisest man who ever lived—King Solomon—who reminded us that there is indeed a time for every contrast in the fabric of life:

a time to be born and a time to die,
a time to plant and a time to uproot,
a time to kill and a time to heal,
a time to tear down and a time to build,
a time to weep and a time to laugh,
a time to mourn and a time to dance,
a time to scatter stones and a time
to gather them,
a time to embrace and a time to refrain,
a time to search and a time to give up,
a time to keep and a time to throw away,
a time to tear and a time to mend,
a time to be silent and a time to speak,
a time to love and a time to hate,
a time for war and a time for peace.
(Eccles. 3:1–8)

Life is full of emotional ups and downs. Most of us have lived long enough to come to expect them. We know there will be days of crying and days of laughter. We just don't expect them to occur in the same day.

The Amish quilters knew all about this and designed a pattern to portray it—Sunshine and Shadow. The Amish living in this country are descendants of immigrants who came from Germany and Switzerland in the eighteenth and nineteenth centuries. Because of their religious beliefs, the Amish live a simple life in harmony with nature, shunning

modern technology invented by "the English," their term for other Americans.[2]

The Amish version of the Sunshine and Shadow quilt uses only bold and vibrant solids in both light and dark colors, since patterned fabric is considered "worldly." Each piece is a small square. The pattern begins with one light-colored square in the middle (sunshine) followed by another row of dark-colored squares (shadow) around that one, followed by another row of sunshine squares around that one, and so forth. The visual effect is one of colors and darkness all working together to portray a beautiful whole.

If all the pieces were merely red and gold and purple and jade and royal, the quilt wouldn't hold the same appeal. But seen in light of the contrasting rows of dark, an interesting picture emerges. A picture of the good with the bad, the light with the dark, or, as my wedding vows state, ". . . for better or for worse, for richer or for poorer, in sickness and in health."

One California woman, who went to live with the Amish for a time, observed, "The Amish love the Sunshine and Shadow quilt pattern. It shows two sides—the dark and light, spirit and form—and the challenge of bringing the two into a larger unity. It's not a choice between extremes: conformity or freedom, discipline or imagination, acceptance or doubt, humility or a raging ego. It's a balancing act that includes opposites."[3]

Balance. That's certainly a word for our day, isn't it? It seems that everyone I talk to is searching for a balance between family, work, ministry, leisure, and the many good things that vie for our attention. And some of us

would consider it a good day if we could just balance our checkbooks!

My daughter, Fiona, has a much better handle on "balance" than her mama. Her personality is even-keeled, and she speaks only when she has something to say. (Imagine!) As a teenager, whenever she noticed my dramatic ups and downs she deadpanned, "Chill, Mom. Chill." And when her dad helped her settle into her freshman dorm one thousand miles from home and got too verbal about some triviality, Fiona calmly stated, "Choose your battles, Dad."

Fiona is artistic and manages to blend the Sunshine and Shadow of her life at Vanderbilt University—being an honor student and also playing rugby; riding for the equestrian club and also participating in InterVarsity Christian Fellowship. So I wasn't terribly surprised when she phoned one week to say that her long, dark brown hair now had a bright streak of hot pink in it.

"Mom, the preacher looked directly at me during his sermon about how people need to know the Lord—just because of my pink hair!" Fiona laughed at this response to the Sunshine and Shadow of her hair color—her own way of balancing the ridiculous with the sublime.

In quilting, it is the balance between the light and dark that develops the emerging picture in the final product. Even the same pattern can be totally changed by simply varying the light and dark pieces.

That's how life is. No two lives are alike. When I'm up, you may be down, and vice versa. Of course I like the bright colors better—I'd far rather be happy than sad. But since that's not the way God made it, I'll keep learning how to "chill" while being thankful for the Sunshine and Shadow in the quilt of my life. At least my life is never boring—it's never gray.

CHAPTER FIVE

MARINER'S COMPASS

I sailed on the last voyage of the *H.M.S. Queen Elizabeth.* When we disembarked, the "old lady" was put in dry dock. (I honestly don't think it had anything to do with me. After all, she had survived worse—World War II, for example.) A few years later, the ship burned in Hong Kong Harbor, where she was spending her retirement years as a floating university. It makes me a bit sad that she wasn't still navigating the high seas to the very end.

Although I don't know much about boats and ships and charting a course, I do remember something my mama used to say: "If you don't know where you're going, you'll get there every time!"

Remember the cartoon about Charlie Brown and Lucy on board a ship? Lucy had unfolded her deck chair but couldn't decide where to put it. "I don't know whether to face front and see where we're going, or to face the rear and see where we've been," she said in exasperation to Charlie Brown.

Charlie, meanwhile, had become all tangled up in his own deck chair and moaned out to Lucy, "I just wish I could get my chair open!"

Do you ever feel that way? You're not even at the point of being concerned about direction; you just want to get in the game. Well, join the human race! We all need a little guidance through the storms of life.

On the sea, where water looks the same as far as the eye can see, compasses are used to point the way. Mariner's Compass is a beautiful quilt pattern that probably originated in New England during the great whaling days, when women were left at home for years at a time while their men went off to sea. They were inspired by the "sixteenth century cartographers who made wonderful sailing charts and let their imaginations run free."[1] I'm sure that many a wife was thankful to know that there were such things as a mariner's compass to guide her husband home.

If you have seen a Mariner's Compass quilt, you will recognize the star designs that radiate from the center of a circle. But did you know that each one has either sixteen or thirty-two points, just like the compass card on a magnetic compass? Judy Mathieson, an expert on this type of quilt, once said, "The most important aspect of the Mariner's Compass construction is accuracy, accuracy, accuracy."[2]

Young people who are seeking God's way often lament (just as I have been known to do), "If only God would just tell me *exactly* whom to marry, *exactly* what job to accept, and *exactly* where to live." In other words, they want to know "the plan" so they can follow it. They, too, want accuracy, accuracy, accuracy.

But sometimes God chooses to merely point the way. In our obedience to the direction he gives, he will work out his complete plan for our lives. You may disagree with me, but I believe when I face God as judge, he will not be quite so concerned with accuracy as he will be with faithfulness. I know there have been times when I have traveled a less-than-best path, but when I remembered to consult the "compass" in my life, God wove my path back into his narrow road.

Madame Guyon, a French Christian from the seventeenth century, also made such an analogy to maritime guidance. She wrote that when sailors first take a ship out of port, it is very difficult to head it out to sea and get it clear of the harbor. But once the ship is at sea, it moves easily in whatever direction the seamen choose. Madame Guyon said that Christians are like that ship. At first we are strongly bound by sin and self. It is only by a great deal of repeated effort that the ropes binding us are set loose, and we are free to head in the direction to which God has called us. "*To spread the sails* is to lay yourself before God in simple prayer. *To spread the sails* is to be moved by His Spirit. *To hold the rudder* is to keep your heart from wandering away from its true course. *To hold the rudder* is to recall the heart, gently. You guide it firmly by the moving of the Spirit of God."[3]

But what about those storms at sea? What do we do when our "boat" is tossed and turned by every wave?

In my own life, I have turned to God to show me the way not only through the storms, but also when I didn't even know which direction to face. With the psalmist I exclaim,

Sometimes God chooses to merely point the way. In our obedience to the direction he gives, he will work out his complete plan for our lives. . . . I know there have been times when I have traveled a less-than-best path, but when I remembered to consult the "compass" in my life, God wove my path back into his narrow road.

Show me your ways, O LORD,
teach me your paths;
guide me in your truth and teach me,
for you are God my Savior,
and my hope is in you all day long. (Ps. 25:4–5)

Twenty years ago I graduated from Gordon-Conwell Theological Seminary, which is perched high on a hill north of Boston. The central focus of the campus is the chapel spire, which is lit up at night. Because it's one of the highest points in the Boston area, many airlines use it as a navigational tool in their landing pattern for Logan Airport. During the early 1970s energy crisis, the seminary decided to conserve on electricity and not light the spire at night. As oral tradition goes, Logan Airport officials phoned in a request to the seminary. That's when it was learned that the light was truly a beacon—giving not only spiritual direction to New England, but navigational guidance as well! Needless to say, the spire was once again lit and has not gone out since.

Thomas Merton wrote a powerful prayer for those of us desperately searching for a beacon of light:

> God, we have no idea where we are going. We do not see the road ahead of us. We cannot know for certain where it will end. Nor do we really know ourselves, and the fact that we think we are following your will does not mean that we are actually doing so. But we believe that the desire to please you does in fact please you. And we hope we have that desire in all that we are doing. We hope that we will never do anything apart from that desire. And we know that if we do this you will lead us by the right road, though we may know nothing about it. Therefore, we will trust you always though we may seem to be lost and in the shadow of death. We will

not fear, for you are ever with us, and you will never leave us to face our perils alone.[4]

You are never alone in your peril. But, like the ill-fated crew of the *Titanic*, we sometimes fail to heed warnings. If God is saying to you, "Look out, there is an iceberg!" then change your course! Don't laugh in his face and reply, "I'm not susceptible to that kind of peril; I'm strong." Even the most touted luxury liner had a weak point, and all the pride, money, and even courage in the world couldn't save those who died on the *Titanic*.

The small New England village where I live also has a tall church spire that is lit every night. You can see it from our home several blocks away. You can see it from Interstate 91 as well as from the site over the bridge that crosses the Connecticut River. You can even see it from the air just before landing at the Hartford/Springfield Airport. When we first moved here, I told my younger children, "If you get lost, just look for the church spire—it will show you the way." Truly, it is like a compass to me, always bringing me home. It guides me to God's house—and to God.

I've been lost before, and I'll probably get lost again when I visit or move to another city. But now I know to look up! The Mariner's Compass has become part of the quilt of my life because it points me to seek God's guidance and then to respond obediently to the directions he gives.

The revelation of Yahweh is whole
and pulls our lives together.

The signposts of Yahweh are clear
and point out the right road.
The life-maps of Yahweh are right,
showing the way to joy.
The directions of Yahweh are plain
and easy on the eyes.
(Ps. 19:7–8 *The Message*)

CHAPTER SIX

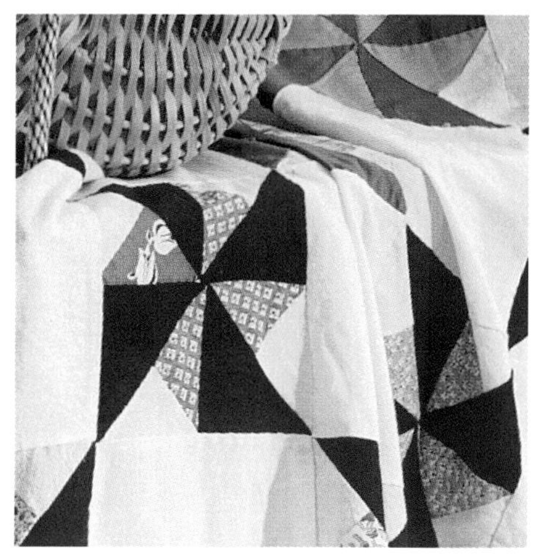

WINDMILL

We wait until the last possible moment. Why we wait I do not know. Is it fear of what emotions might be stirred? Or is it just because we want to avoid any infusion of melancholy into our two-week holiday in the Netherlands?

I suppose the reasons don't matter so much. What matters is that we are leaving Holland tomorrow, and there is one very important task yet to be accomplished.

We drive past the old windmill and park near the Saint Willibrord Kerk cemetery, which dates back to the eighth century. It is named after an English priest named Willibrord who set out to convert the fierce and pagan Frisians in what

is today known as the Netherlands. He established a strong and dedicated "beachhead" at Utrecht, where he eventually became archbishop.[1] Into this historic churchyard, each of our four children carries a pot of beautiful Dutch perennials while my husband carries a shiny new spade bought especially for the occasion.

As we walk together, I silently wonder how many families over the past thirteen hundred years have traveled this same path to pay tribute to long-departed loved ones. More specifically, how many women like me have come to visit the grave of their husband's first wife?

Inka Van Seventer and Mike McDowell met at L'Abri, a refuge in Switzerland that welcomed seekers of Christian truth. Both found there a place to study, work, pray, and learn from its founders, Francis and Edith Schaeffer. After Francis Schaeffer performed their wedding ceremony in Holland, Mike and Inka returned to seminary in the United States. Then they served with InterVarsity Christian Fellowship, ministering to university students in Seattle. God gave them three children—Justin, Timothy, and Fiona.

Soon after their tenth wedding anniversary, Inka died of liver cancer. Fiona was one year old; the boys were six and four. Two weeks prior to Inka's death, Mike moved his little family to Holland so Inka could spend her last days near her parents and six siblings.

Now, sixteen years later, we are in the ancient *Gronekerk* cemetery where she is buried. Because they were so young, Inka's children have little primary memory of her; however, we and her other family members have sought to acquaint them with her through stories, photographs, and mementos.

Fourteen years ago when I married Mike, I chose to legally adopt Justin, Timothy, and Fiona. Though I am not their birth mother, I am their mother. With a large dose of God's grace, I have been greatly privileged to raise them and their little sister Maggie.

Today they are young adults, and Mike and I feel it is important for them as adults to have these moments at "Mommy Inka's" grave. Important for whom? Well, only time will tell if it will be a touchstone for them or not. But we want to show them this place—to talk about Inka, answer their questions, and thank God for her life—in the shadow of the old Oegstgeest windmill.

Windmills seem to be the universal symbol for the tiny country of the Netherlands, especially the old-fashioned windmills made of wood and canvas. Nonetheless, today's wind power plants are arrays of sleek metal wind turbines that you see everywhere dotting the landscape—along with the tulips of course.

Having clusters of windmills (or *gangs* as the Dutch called those early wind farms) is nothing new. Only by tapping the power of multiple windmills could Jan Leeghwater (his name means literally "empty water") and the engineers who followed him drain the polders and make the Netherlands what it is today—a country built on land reclaimed from the sea.

Of course, as I tour the countryside and see the windmills, I am reminded of the Windmill Quilt pattern. It is made by cutting four squares of a light four-patch and those of a dark four-patch diagonally across and then combining the resulting triangles in an alternating color arrangement. If one stares at the design for a while, all the

little windmills seem to revolve and give a pinwheel effect. Once again, the principle of all the little pieces working together to form the whole picture applies here in a beautiful way.

Holland is Inka's homeland and the country where her family still lives—a family that has become very important in my own life. Because of the dense population of this small area of land, each grave site is three people deep. We explain this to the children as they discover not one, but three tombstone markers on the grave. Inka's mother and father—their Oma and Opa—died after her, and this is their grave also.

The burial site is not merely a slab, as so often happens in the United States, but a walled garden! And even though there are many plants and flowers here already, each of our children finds a spot to plant their special one.

We work in silence, occasionally filling up the watering pail at the cemetery well. All finished, we gather in a circle and Mike leads us in prayer. As he begins to thank God for Inka's life, he sounds very much like the minister he is. But halfway through the prayer he transitions to the man—the one who loved her and has carried on faithfully with their family in her absence. Tears come all too easily today for Mike and me.

Justin is now a young man of twenty-two, an overcomer. He prays from the heart: "Dear Lord, thank you for Mommy Inka. I know she was a good mom. I know she took care of me. She fed me. She dressed me. She helped me. I'm sorry she died. Amen." My heart swells. I had heard that one of Inka's greatest concerns was the future of her oldest son who was born with mental retardation. And yet here he

is, a wonderful, articulate young man who has offered this prayer as his greatest gift and tribute to his first mom.

Tim and Fiona say their prayers silently. Maggie—age eight and the only one of my children who shares my genes—weeps a bit and says, "I wish Mommy Inka didn't have to die." (Later the impact of this will sink in, and she will return to me with the inevitable question, "But if Mommy Inka hadn't died, who would have been my daddy?" Her question is certainly something to ponder.)

It's time to go. I feel as though a torch has been passed. I doubt all six of us will ever gather together here in this spot across the sea again. But I suspect there may be more visits here eventually. We have shown the way, and truly that is all any parent can ever do.

Tonight we will join many of our Dutch relatives for a celebratory pancake supper before we fly home—the Windmill pattern is finally stitched into place in the quilt of my own life.

CHAPTER SEVEN

LOG CABIN

I was born in a house that had a name. No, it wasn't a mansion or an English country estate. It was just a regular house in a Southern town. The name of the place was Pinecrest. You see, my parents (who moved into the house the day after they married) took one look at all the tall Georgia pine trees, added it to the family name—Secrest—and our home was christened Pinecrest.

In subsequent years, we had other homes with such names as Brookside and Quiet Place (that was certainly a misnomer!). All were inspired. Brookside was a farm with—you guessed it—a brook on either boundary. Quict Placc was named thus because my daddy bought it just after his brain surgery when

he kept hearing the line from a gospel hymn—*"There is a quiet place, far from the rapid pace"*—during his hallucinations. No joke.

I can't document this scientifically, but houses with names seem to reach out and embrace you. Sometimes they even live up to their names. My husband found spiritual shelter during the turbulent 1970s in Francis and Edith Schaeffer's Swiss home, L'Abri, which is also the French word for "shelter." My colleagues, Jey and Joan Deifell, are thankful for every moment they can retreat to their mountain cabin called Rest and Be Thankful, named after a mountain pass in the Scottish highlands. Some dear friends on Cape Cod, the Rowes, have christened their home Rowes' Garden, where their five children are currently blossoming.

People have always wanted the comfort and security of a home. Unfortunately, pioneer women often had to settle for precious little in that area. Those covered wagons were pretty bumpy, and you can just imagine living in a sod house—a house made of bits of mud. (How do you clean house when it's mud to begin with?)

By the time a pioneer family gained enough stability to build a solid structure, log cabins looked pretty good to them—chinks and all. No wonder the Log Cabin quilt pattern, first introduced between 1810 and 1830, continues to be an all-time favorite. In fact, due to President Abraham Lincoln's "Log Cabin Campaign," it became a popular pattern after the Civil War, representing pioneer stalwartness and American individualism. During those years, many Log Cabin quilt contests were held at county fairs.[1]

You've probably seen Log Cabin quilts, but every time you do, they may look different. That's because the pattern is made

just like the cabins, log upon log upon log. It begins with a square center, often called the "chimney," that is portrayed in red to symbolize a warm fire. Four "logs" graduated in length are built up on each of its four sides. The quilt block is carefully shaded, with half of the logs being light colors and the other half dark colors. By varying the light and dark color locations, you can change the overall view of the completed quilt picture. These variations even have their own names: Log Cabin Barn Raising, Log Cabin Streak O' Lightning, Log Cabin Courthouse Steps, or Log Cabin Straight Furrow.

Just as Log Cabin quilters act as builders, fitting long and short logs together into a perfect square, so do those of us who consider ourselves "homemakers" (whether men or women); we also become builders of a sort: We build atmosphere; we build belonging; we build lives. We fit together the material and the immaterial pieces of our lives. "Home is where memories and possessions become one. Laughter shared and tears consoled are instantly recalled with the hum of the furnace and the smells from the kitchen. Secret places and hidden emotions are all safely tucked away within reach. Every object speaks to your personality, and all the truly important people in your life have shared this sanctuary. Love is the single ingredient that transforms your dwelling into a home."[2]

Did you grow up in a place that made you feel safe? Even if you didn't, wouldn't you like your own children to be launched from what they consider a "home" out into the world each day?

The psalmist turned to God for his home of safety: "Keep me safe, O God, for in you I take refuge" (Ps. 16:1). What

does it take to build your own "Log Cabin," figuratively speaking? It takes more than just giving it a name—but that's a start.

My husband and I always give our houses names, even if we just rent. Many folk don't own the house they live in, but that's no reason not to try and infuse as much of you into it as you can.

Our house in the Blue Ridge mountains was named High Hopes. Not only were we at a pretty high altitude, we were also full of hope for the future. When the time came for us to move into a 1924 parsonage in New England, God was teaching us about grace, so we christened it Gracehaven. Our prayer at that time was to receive God's grace so that we could extend grace to others—beginning with our own children but also establishing a haven for others who came.

This is our eighth year at Gracehaven. During that time, I have learned far more about grace than I have passed on, I'm sure. God has shown me that *grace* is a gift from him that I can never earn—as well as one I can never lose. When I fully embrace his unconditional love for me, I am then to become a grace-giver to others.

As part of my legacy to my four children, I wrote twelve important lessons I've learned during the first half of my life and dedicated the book to them—*Amazed by Grace.*[3] In that book I shared some good news for all Christians: we don't have to keep trying harder to please God. Instead, we are privileged to bask in his unconditional love as sons and daughters.

Grace, God's grace, is our emotional home. As Paul said, "Since we have been justified through faith, we have peace with God through our Lord Jesus Christ, through whom we

have gained access by faith into this grace in which we now stand. And we rejoice in the hope of the glory of God" (Rom. 5:1–2). Knowing that we are already loved, already accepted, and already children of the divine Landlord gives us a true home—a secure haven.

Therefore, even a Log Cabin can seem like a castle—if it is a place where we know we are accepted and loved. "He who dwells in the shelter of the Most High will rest in the shadow of the Almighty" (Ps. 91:1).

When my friend Ingrid Trobisch was widowed, she moved back to Missouri and named her new home *Haus Geborgenheit*, which is German for "place of steadfast shelter." I am grateful to her for teaching me much about the importance of creating a sense of emotional safety in a home. In her book *Keeper of the Springs*, she said,

> Perhaps the greater the Shelter of family feeling children experience growing up, the more they'll miss it when it's not there, and as adults, the harder they'll work to create it around their own hearth. Those who have never had it may crave it more deeply yet. I see many people hungry for this. Perhaps each one of us need more places in our lives with a wing-back chair where we can nestle on our Heavenly Father's lap.
>
> By allowing vulnerable experiences in quiet and rest, you become a person who makes every context a safe place. Your life becomes Shelter—whether giving a good-night kiss to a child or listening to the secret dreams of a spouse.[4]

Look around you today. What would it take to transform the place you live (whether apartment, trailer, condominium, retirement center, or even mansion) into a refuge—a sanctuary from which you can draw strength to go forth and face the world, a resting place for your heart and your soul? Begin by spending time with God and asking him to quiet you and help you know the things that are the most important. Then look at making your *home* a wonderful calling.

Contemporary artist Thomas Kinkade has painted his fair share of log cabins, and all of them appear to have warm inviting lights in the windows. That's because Kinkade is an *illuminist,* a "painter of light." He also knows the hunger people have for a haven, a safe place:

> I hear the yearning almost every day from people who talk or write to me about my paintings. "That's where I want to be," they say of a scene I've depicted. "I want to step into that painting, walk down that path, and live in that house with the glowing windows."
>
> Obviously, they don't really want to live in a painting. They are simply desiring the world of peace and simplicity I try to portray in my work. They are yearning for a life that focuses on what is truly important and what is truly beautiful—a life that is different from the rushed, cluttered existence our popular culture promotes.
>
> There is nothing wrong with that kind of yearning. It's my yearning, too, and the reason I paint the kind

of scenes I do. In fact, I believe something has gone seriously wrong if we don't have that kind of hunger for a better, simpler way of life. Human beings were not made for the rush-hour, freeway kind of life we try so frantically to live. We were made for calm, not chaos, and that is why we long for simpler times. Somewhere deep inside we know that simpler times are better times.

That's the kind of life I strive to evoke in my paintings. It's the kind of life I'm committed to building for myself and my family. And it's the foundational message I want to share with the world through my work and through my life.[5]

Like Kinkade, each of us has a "foundational message" that we project to those around us—whether intentionally or unwittingly. The world desperately needs a message of hope, haven, and hospitality. With God's help, I gratefully stitch the homespun simplicity of the Log Cabin in the quilt of my own life.

CHAPTER EIGHT

EYE OF GOD

For years our kids insisted they were the only ones on the planet who had never been to Disney World. They weren't even comforted when I pointed out that most children in Third World countries had never even heard of Disney. But because I understood their desires, I entered contests. I figured someone had to win those "all-expenses-paid" family trips. Why not us?

I never won a trip.

By the time we finally were able to go to Disney World (in other words, I had a speaking engagement down there during winter break), our two sons were in their twenties and in college. So we took our daughters—one a high school

senior and one a second-grader. We also took along our teenager's best friend. (I had been advised that this was the only way to maintain sanity with having a teenage girl stuck with her family on vacation. Good advice!)

We bought passes that let us hit a different kingdom every day and tried to squeeze in as much as we could before our legs—or our money—gave out. Of course, we had a blast. Yet whenever someone asks me, "What was your favorite sight at Disney World?" my answer comes quickly: "My daughter's face."

I spent the whole time watching Maggie enjoy all the fantasy and excitement and glamour and glitz Disney had to offer. Amidst all those distractions, the one sight my eyes sought out was her. I think God is a lot like that.

The world seeks to entertain, tempt, dazzle, and impress, but God's eyes are always on the lookout for the most incredible sight of all—*me*, his daughter! His love for me is far better than any love I once dreamed of while listening to that old Lettermen song, "You're just too good to be true; can't take my eyes off of you."

When I was in seminary, I learned all the hundred-dollar words that describe God's character, words like *omniscient* and *omnipotent* and *omnipresent*. They're good to know when you need to establish credibility in a denominational meeting, but more often than not I prefer to simply state the obvious: God is keeping an eye on me because he loves me that much.

The fact of God's constant vigilance must have been a special comfort to the pioneer women who first named this quilt pattern Eye of God. They were isolated on a vast prairie

in a harsh land that all too often took their youth, their babies, and their dreams. Usually the only book available was the family Bible, and these women consoled themselves with verses such as these:

From heaven the Lord looks down
and sees all mankind;
from his dwelling place he watches
all who live on earth—
he who forms the hearts of all,
who considers everything they do.
(Ps. 33:13–14)
The Lord watches over all who love him.
(Ps. 145:20)

What comfort they must have known to think of God looking down on them with loving eyes. And, just as picking up a tiny square of cloth doesn't give us the total picture of the quilt in process, what we see going on in our own lives doesn't always reveal the total picture. Although the author of the following poem is unknown, this poet knew that perspective makes a difference:

The Loom of Time

Man's life is laid in the loom of time
To a pattern he does not see,
While the weavers work and the shuttles fly
Till the dawn of eternity.

Some shuttles are filled with silver threads
And some with threads of gold,

While often but the darker hues
Are all that they may hold.

But the Weaver watches with skillful eye
Each shuttle fly to and fro,
And sees the pattern so deftly wrought
As the loom moves sure and slow.
God surely planned the pattern:
Each thread, the dark and fair,
Is chosen by His master skill
And placed in the web with care.

He only knows its beauty,
And guides the shuttles which hold
The threads so unattractive,
As well as threads of gold.
Not till each loom is silent,
And the shuttles cease to fly,
Shall God reveal the pattern
And explain the reason why

The dark threads were as needful
In the Weaver's skillful hand
As the threads of gold and silver
For the pattern which He planned. [1]

My friend Linda Riley knows the Eye of God has a special perspective that we can't always see from where we are. In a much crumpled letter I've saved for years, her words jump out at me even today: "God is good and only does good. When it doesn't look that way, it's only because *heaven's true*

perspective cannot be achieved from Earth's vantage point. We rarely glimpse even fragments of the whole fantastic tableau of beautiful patterns God weaves through time and space."[2]

As the quilt of Linda's life has unfolded, God's patchwork pattern has become more and more clear. She and her husband, Jay, married young, but by their tenth anniversary, there were no children. Their only arguments had been about whether or not they would name their first daughter Autumn (Linda's choice) or Amanda (Jay's choice). However, the daughter hadn't come. As Linda said, "God did not appear to be on the job. He had failed to fulfill our 'order.' We went to the Complaint Department, all to no avail. Then we went to Plan B."

They decided to adopt a sibling group. During the time of waiting, Linda and Jay prayed for God to put their family together. One day, Los Angeles County Adoptions called them with the news that two sisters, ages three and five, had been relinquished by their mother. Though not a believer herself, she had requested the girls be put in a Christian family.

The soon-to-be-parents asked the social worker to tell them more about the girls. They heard these remarkable words: "They're both green-eyed blondes. The five-year-old is named Autumn. The three-year-old is named Amanda."

And, as if that weren't enough, Autumn's middle name was Marie, Linda's middle name; and Amanda's middle name was Linn, the nickname that all Linda's family and closest friends call her.

The God who is in control once again showed two of his precious children that his eye had been on them and that his

pattern would unfold in their sight in due time. Linda concluded the letter, "While I was crying over my barrenness, my babies were carried and born. While God seemed silent and uncaring, He was at work in His own magnificent way."[3]

Do you ever feel too small to be seen by God? Sometimes I think of all the major crises he must deal with each day—wars and famines and earthquakes. Through the smoke and fire, can he even see li'l ole me down here in this snow-covered New England village?

Jesus used a wonderful word picture to show people like you and me how significant we are to the heavenly Father: "Are not two sparrows sold for a penny? Yet not one of them will fall to the ground apart from the will of your Father. . . . So don't be afraid; you are worth more than many sparrows" (Matt. 10:29, 31). In Psalm 84, the psalmist cried out for the living God and exclaimed, "Even the sparrow has found a home, . . . a place near your altar, O Lord Almighty, my King and my God" (v. 3).

Truly we can join in the chorus of saints who sing that wonderful old spiritual *"His eye is on the sparrow, and I know he watches me."*

Do you ever wonder what God sees when he looks down on you? Mack Thomas captured the concept of the Eye of God perfectly in his book for children of all ages, *Through the Eyes of Jesus*:

> I see you. Right now I'm looking at you, and I always see you, every moment. I see every step you take. I see everything you hold in your hand. I see every thought you have in your mind. I know you. I know all about

you. I knew it all before you were even born. Before you took your first breath, I knew what would happen on every day of your life. I know all of your secrets. I know all your plans. I know everything you wish for and hope for. I know what makes you happy.

I know everything you're afraid of. I know everything you're worried about. I know your every hurt. I know what makes you angry. I know what makes you sad. I see you. I know you. I love you.

I love you. And because I love you, I know you. And because I know you—I will never let you out of my sight.[4]

I am so thankful for the Eye of God watching over me, his child, as the quilt of my life unfolds. How about you?

The LORD watches . . .
the LORD is your shade . . .
The LORD will keep you . . .
he will watch over . . .
The LORD will watch over . . .
both now and forevermore.(Ps. 121:5, 7)

CHAPTER NINE

SUNBONNET SUE

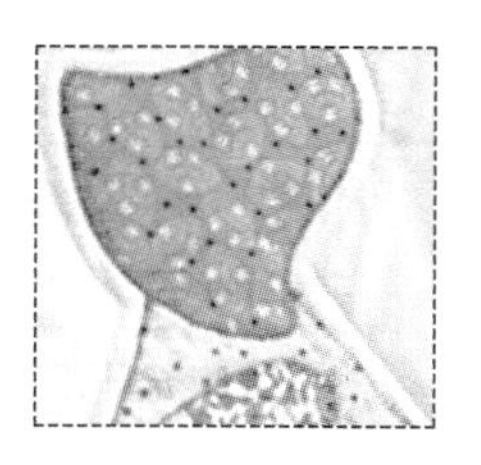

We're sitting around in our jammies, gathering quilts or comforters around us as we chat, twelve women ages thirty-eight to fifty-eight. No one has on makeup; most of us have a few tearstains as well as some new laugh wrinkles from an earlier session, and all of us are being refreshingly honest.

Is this the latest New Age women's therapy group? No. It is a group, of sorts, and if encouragement and prayerful support can be called *therapy*, then it is a therapy group. Since the word "therapy" is derived from the Greek word *therapeuo*, which means "to serve," "to restore," or "to care for," then in that sense we are therapists to one another

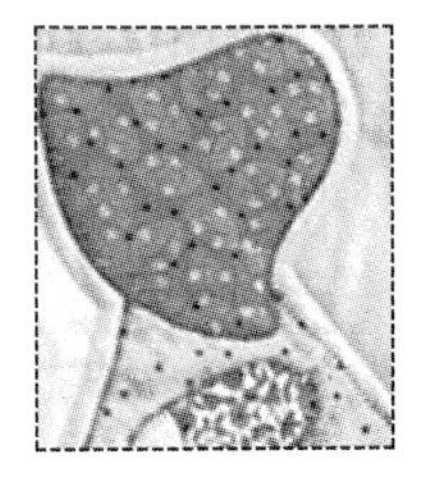

because our relationships are characterized by serving and caring.

We are not cookie-cutter copies of one another, but we do have at least two things in common: we're all followers of Jesus Christ, and we all have a public voice through our speaking and writing. We call ourselves a circle, because we're not an organization with a leader; we are peers—sisters who have joined together because we know we can't go it alone.

Years ago when we found each other, we adopted the handle "Heartspring," claiming the Scripture: "For out of the overflow of [her] heart, [her] mouth speaks" (Luke 6:45). As sinners saved by grace, we knew we had to guard our hearts above all things (see Prov. 4:23) so that God might use us through the power of his Spirit to draw others to a closer relationship with him.

Once a year we gather in a beautiful seaside home (run by the Sisters of Mercy) to simply be together and draw strength from one another and our merciful Lord. You might look at us as sort of a Sunbonnet Sue quilt—you know, that pattern where there are usually twelve or sixteen appliquéd girls in large bonnets all facing the same way. Each has clothing made from a variety of fabric, but they are joined together by a complementary sashing in between each quilt square.

I wonder if Depression-era women developed the Sunbonnet Sue pattern as a result of their socials together around a quilting frame. During those ten years from 1929 to 1939, times were so lean that quilts were made primarily from sackcloth scraps of feed, flour, and sugar sack prints. "Sue had her origins in the Sunbonnet Babies primers of the late nineteenth century, some of which are still available

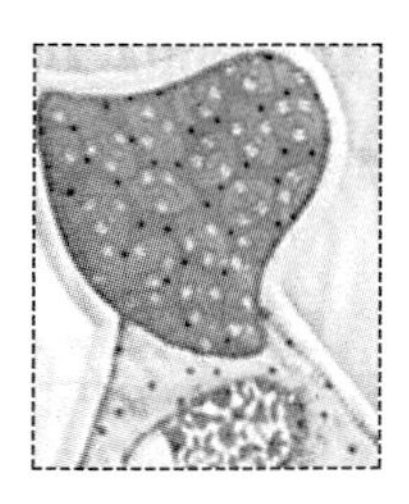

in reprint. She was depicted on quilts from early in the twentieth century, an industrious little girl doing all the chores that all children were expected to participate in at that time."[1] My mama still treasures the Sunbonnet Sue quilt made from feed sacks by her grandmother when she was only about five years old.

Although Sunbonnet Sue is a pattern from the early twentieth century, the "sisterhood" that it portrays had been foundational for at least a hundred years prior. Life was lonely for our hard-working foremothers who seemed to age overnight with the worry of the world on their shoulders. One of their few social pleasures was the opportunity to bring fabric scraps together and share in a quilting bee while the menfolk were busy raising a barn or some such thing.

Pioneer women particularly appreciated the cooperative effort of quilting as soon as they had neighbors: "Historians of the West have emphasized how important it was for women to create female support systems, co-operative networks in newly settled areas. Women suffered more than men from the settlement patterns that characterized the West—far-flung farms or homesteads miles distant from the nearest neighbors and from towns. . . . With their former female world ruptured, women had to create a new one: it was part of creating an environment, that domestic-cultural space within which they existed . . . They depended upon each other for physical, psychological and emotional support."[2]

Did they share concerns about the spiritual lives of their children? Did they talk about how hard it was to get their husbands to talk to them about the things that really mattered? Did they offer advice on how to make ends meet

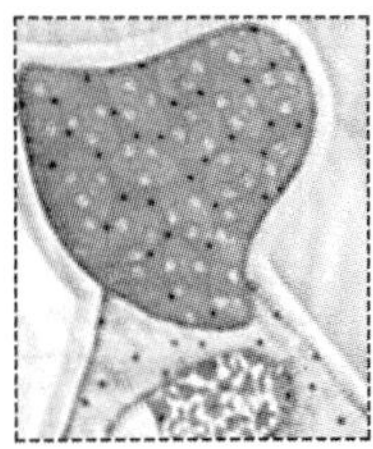

when the crops failed and there were no jobs available in the cities? Did they cry on one another's shoulder as babies died year after year after year? And after everyone departed, did they remember one another in prayer?

I think quilting bees were definitely one of the forerunners of the modern-day small groups. Women were eager to get together in a safe environment where they could speak about issues of interest to them and exchange ideas with others. Even the names of their quilt patterns were often politically or biblically motivated to get across their message. For many years, this was the only way they could speak out against such things as alcohol or slavery and speak for such things as a woman's right to vote. Even Susan B. Anthony first spoke out in favor of women's suffrage at a meeting of quilters.

Political quilts made by women at quilting bees in the nineteenth century depicted political elections and problems that concerned these women who had no other public voice. They found an outlet for expression through their quilts made in the domestic sphere to which they were confined.

Jinny Beyer, affectionately referred to by her friends as "the Martha Stewart of quilting," believes in the importance of quilting groups today. "I think one of the things that people like about quilting is just sitting and sewing and chatting. I mean, I've always thought of it as a group therapy session. When you meet in the smaller bees, you have that opportunity to just sit and talk things out."[3]

I consider one of my earlier books, *Women's Spiritual Passages*,[4] as a sort of Sunbonnet Sue quilt. In it are the stories of fifty women who have just crossed that marvelous threshold we call "the big 4-0." With amazing honesty, each one tells a

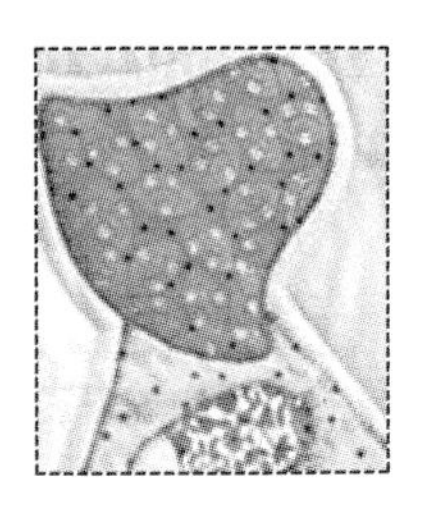

specific lesson she has learned in life thus far. And what a forum for speaking out on aspects of life, loss, and love! Almost weekly I receive letters from women who have read these stories and identified with the vulnerability of those who related God's faithfulness along their journey so far.

Women need other women. The Charlottesville, Virginia, Quilt Guild points out that the last twenty-five years have seen a revival of quilting groups, and "whether their most important aspect is the quilt or the group is a moot point. As we've seen with the coffee klatch of the 50s, the women's groups of the 60s and 70s, the New Girl Networks of the 80s and the 'girlfriend' movement of the 90s, women have a need to get together with other women, to get and give their support to each other."[5]

That's why I love being involved in women's ministry through my own church and by speaking to women across the country. Bible studies, mothers' groups, prayer groups, women's circles, and even recovery groups are all places where the Spirit of God and the spirit of belonging can help women put the pieces of their fractured lives back together again.

Both in my weekly early morning prayer group, "Daybreak," and in my covenant group, "Heartspring," we try to follow some guidelines for our special time and relationship. Accountability has freer reign when there are promises, or covenants, between those involved. These particular ideas were shared years ago by Louis Evans Jr. and have been tried and tested in many groups:

1. The covenant of affirmation (unconditional love)
2. The covenant of availability

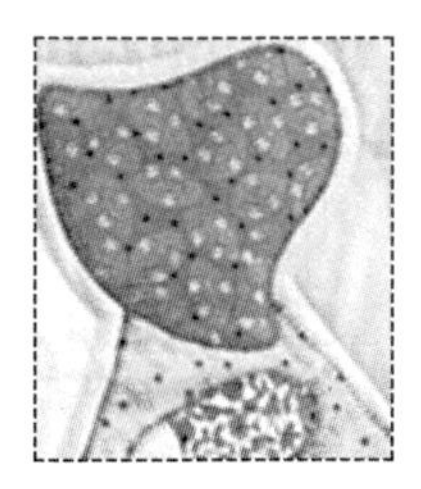

3. The covenant of prayer
4. The covenant of openness
5. The covenant of honesty
6. The covenant of sensitivity
7. The covenant of confidentiality
8. The covenant of accountability[6]

Many of us are afraid that if others really knew us, they wouldn't like us. But if you have ever been in a group where fellow members strive to love you honestly and challenge you with love and sacrificial service, then you have experienced the true comfort of knowing and being known.

Quilt lover and Pulitzer-Prize-winning author Anna Quindlan writes that when she looks at a quilt, she sees "a circle of women, building it bit by bit, block by block, and as they do so talking to one another, about their days and their disappointments, their husbands and their children, the food they cook and the houses they furnish and the dreams they dream. . . . I imagine all of mine, no matter what their pattern, are emblems of female friendship, that essential thread that has so often kept the pieces of my own life together, and from time to time kept me from falling apart."[7]

Do you have friends like that? Are you a friend like that?

Quindlan goes on to say, "Piece by piece we stitch the world together into something we can work with, something

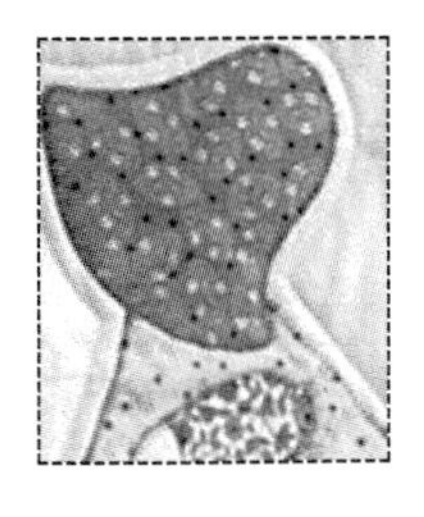

with which we can cover ourselves against the cold nights. I don't know what in the world I would do without them, for advice, for comfort, for simply knowing that there is someone out there who knows me as I am, and loves me despite and because of it."[8]

Acceptance is important, but for the Christian woman there is also the added dimension of prayer support. Perhaps the most important gift my "Heartspring" sisters give to me is the gift of intercessory prayer. Each of us carries around a calendar upon which are the dates and plans of all twelve of us. On any given day I might be praying for someone speaking to a group in California, or another teaching photography in New Zealand, or someone else finishing a book manuscript in Massachusetts. And whatever I am doing that day is also remembered by them.

Friends are precious. As soon as I finish this book, I hope to complete my own Sunbonnet Sue sewing project. What a reminder of those covenant sisters who all stand beside me as we face the future together! We echo Ruth's words to Naomi: "Where you go I will go, and where you stay I will stay. Your people will be my people and your God my God" (Ruth 1:16).

CHAPTER TEN

BROKEN DISHES

I'm not much of a shopper. But occasionally I run across a bazaar or thrift shop with cast-off pieces of china. I love picking through those collections, now tossed aside, but once so lovingly treasured by someone's Great Aunt Lavinia.

Since I collect teapots and teacups, I'm always on the lookout for something unique. But having little money to support this habit, I am often relegated to the back tables containing merchandise marked "as is." That usually means that the seller knows about the cracks and chips and wants you to know that the price on it reflects such things. In other words, don't try to barter or point out blemishes hoping for a better deal.

I have a lot of "as is" china dishes. I'm eccentric enough to believe the cracks and chips just give them character. *I don't need my dishes to be perfect in order to enjoy them. Broken dishes can still be used, you know.*

Do you suppose God knew that when he allowed me to become the mother of a child born with mental retardation? First of all, let me make it clear that I don't consider my son Justin "broken" at all. He is, in fact, one of the most "whole" people I have ever known, if you are looking on the soul and self-image. In fact, perhaps the greatest act of grace in my life is that this special son has grown up truly believing that he is a child of God, made in God's image, with tremendous worth.

When I occasionally remark to him, "Justin, I sure like being with you. You're great company," he simply smiles sheepishly and replies, "I know." It's not a boast, simply an affirmation that what I have said is indeed true.

I have learned a lot in the twenty-plus years that I have cared deeply about those with disabilities. In the forefront of my acquired evaluation is every indication that most of the general public sees people who have special physical or mental needs as not completely whole—Broken Dishes, if you will.

Yet all humans are created in the image of God! Even Saint Augustine went against the thinking of his day by declaring all men thus: "But no faithful Christian should doubt that anyone who is born anywhere as a man—that is, a rational and mortal being—derives from that one first-created human being. And this is true, however extraordinary such a creature may appear to our senses in bodily

shape, in colour, or motion, or utterance, or in any natural endowment, or part, or quality."[1]

Unfortunately, even in today's society of political correctness, many do not view those with special needs as created in the image of God. The "something missing" is more apparent to them than the "something there." And those who worship at the altar of success and perfection have little use for lives that appear to have a piece missing here and there.

That's one reason I appreciate quilters so much. Quilters can look at scraps of material, pieces of worn-out clothing—even old feed sacks—and envision not only how they can be used but also how they can be *beautiful* in their use. The Broken Dishes pattern consists of lots of small triangles that come together to form a perfect square. The squares then come together to complete the patchwork picture. It is beautiful, but the end product may turn out somewhat differently than what was originally conceived in the quilter's mind.

Parents of children born with handicaps often feel initially that their dreams have been shattered. And yet I can say from experience that God will replace those dreams—those hopes and expectations—with something more, something entirely different.

When Emily Pearl Kingsley is asked to describe the experience of raising a child with a disability, she likens the expectancy of birth with planning a vacation. She points out that in planning a trip to Italy, you would buy a bunch of guidebooks, make plans to see the Coliseum, and learn a few Italian phrases. But after packing and departure, imagine your surprise when the plane lands and someone says, "Welcome to Holland."

You'd be understandably confused. You had signed up for Italy. All your life you had dreamed of Italy. Then someone changed the plans and you've landed in Holland, and there you must stay.

But, remember, you haven't been taken to a *terrible* place, just a different one than you expected. As Emily says, "So you must go out and buy new guidebooks. And you must learn a whole new language. And you will meet a whole new group of people you otherwise would never have met." However, the problem is: everyone else keeps bragging about a trip to Italy, making you feel that you've missed out on something.

Emily concludes her analogy with these words: "The pain of that will never, ever go away because the loss of that dream is a significant loss. But if you spend your life mourning the fact that you didn't get to Italy, you may never be free to enjoy the very special and very lovely things about Holland."[2]

Did you know that quilters always intentionally make one flaw in each of their quilts? They do that to remind themselves that only God makes all things perfect. But the flaw doesn't make the quilt any less beautiful. We are reminded in 1 Peter 4:10 that each and all of us has been given different gifts: "Each one should use whatever gift he has received to serve others, faithfully administering God's grace in its various forms."

I believe that Broken Dishes can still be used.

Last year our son Justin returned from his first experience with a Prison Fellowship team from our church who visits the youth correctional center each Sunday to lead worship and small-group Bible study. Mike and I could tell he was

very excited as he exclaimed, "Mom and Dad, I know what I can do! I can't preach like you, Dad, and I can't teach and write like you, Mom, but I know what I can do! *I can tell prisoners about Jesus!*"

That was truly an epiphany for him, and for us. God broke through and showed Justin just where he could be used. To this day he continues to go faithfully and share God's answers in his simple faith.

What's more, the prisoners respond to him! They know that he, too, has experienced how it feels to be "different." Perhaps they see in him the opportunity to overcome—with God's help. As the apostle Paul says in 2 Corinthians 1:3–4, "Praise be to the God and Father of our Lord Jesus Christ, the Father of compassion and the God of all comfort, who comforts us in all our troubles, so that we can comfort those in any trouble with the comfort we ourselves have received from God. For just as the sufferings of Christ flow over into our lives, so also through Christ our comfort overflows."

Joni Eareckson Tada certainly wasn't planning to "visit Holland" when she went diving and broke her neck thirty years ago, thereby becoming a quadriplegic. But she, too, has discovered what God has called her to do—to share his faithfulness and hope with disabled people. For example, she relates, "When I was on the platform at the Billy Graham Crusade in Moscow, my interpreter was a blind student from the Moscow State University. He told me it was amazing that God would use a paralyzed woman and a blind boy to put forth the gospel. I believe God delights in using what looks like the shipwrecked, the home wrecked, the poor, unlovely, palsied, elderly. He's using people the

world would never pick for the job. With God, the weak can push back the darkness."[3]

V. Raymond Edman, former president of Wheaton College, was fond of reminding his students that in God's economy, broken is often better. He states, "I have been reflecting on the inestimable value of broken things. Broken pitchers give ample light for victory (Judg. 7:19–21). Broken bread was more than enough for all the hungry (Matt. 14:19–21). A broken box gave fragrance to all the world (Mark 14:3–9). A broken body is salvation to all who believe and receive the Savior (Isa. 53:5–6, 12 and 1 Cor. 11:24). What cannot the broken One do with our broken plans, projects and hearts?"[4]

Years later, one of his students, author Elisabeth Elliot, told me that she would always remember something Dr. Edman told her: "If your life is broken when offered to God, that's because pieces would feed a multitude whereas a loaf could only satisfy a lad."[5] When Elisabeth shared this with me in the context of a discussion on suffering, I began for the first time in my life to embrace my own brokenness and offer it back to God for his glory.

You see, there are broken pieces in all our lives, whether seen or unseen. For the first part of my life I hoped it would be through my strengths that God would use me to spread his love. But I have learned now, in embracing my brokenness, that it is through my weaknesses that God has chosen to give hope to others. If he can work in me, then his faithfulness will certainly be there for you too!

I am reminded of the importance of attitude by Victor Frankl, who wrote from a barracks next to a gas chamber where families were being murdered. Frankl said, "We can't

be responsible for our circumstances, but the one thing no one can take away is our will to choose our attitude in those circumstances. God wants us simply to be faithful."

Judy Squier, a radiant Christian who was born with no legs, wrote the following in a letter to the family of a little boy born without arms and legs: "I am convinced without a doubt that a loving heavenly Father oversees the creative miracles in the inner sanctum of each mother's womb (Psalm 139), and that in His sovereignty there are no accidents. What the caterpillar calls the end of the world, the Creator calls a butterfly. As humanity, we see only the imperfect underside of God's tapestry of our lives. What we judge to be 'tragic—the most dreaded thing that could happen,' I expect we'll one day see as the awesome reason for the beauty and uniqueness of our life and family."[6]

On the coast of Connecticut is a wonderful retreat home called Seascape—a place I go to occasionally to spend time with God and to draw strength and wholeness for the battles I must face. I remember fondly the first time I walked into the Seascape kitchen and noticed the wall above the stove. I was shocked. The plaster wall contains hundreds of remnants of Broken Dishes.

In time, however, the beauty of that wall has worked its way into my soul. Many china patterns are represented as well as a variety of sizes and shapes. All have been secured into the plaster, and together those chards form a beautiful mosaic. Someone took what appeared to be useless throwaways and found a use. Those broken dishes minister to me each time I visit Seascape. I am reminded of the Broken Dishes pattern in the quilt of my own life.

CHAPTER ELEVEN

STAR OF BETHLEHEM

Looking up into the dark sky, I see only one star shining through the haze. It is the North Star, I'm sure—the one that has been used to guide so many. It's cold here in New England, and the forecast is for a "White Christmas." There is already some snow on the ground, but the sky seems far too clear for potential precipitation.

I wonder.

I know it didn't snow on the first Christmas in that Middle Eastern village of Bethlehem, but living in New England, my Christmases now do resemble the Currier and Ives images from long ago. I rarely take time to look up at the stars, but

tonight all I can think about is that first Christmas and that one remarkable Star of Bethlehem.

It was in the 1830s that women first began piecing together quilts with the Star of Bethlehem pattern—one of the few pieced patterns to come to us from Europe. Today it is still one of the most popular patterns to make—one huge, eight-pointed, multipieced star covering the entire quilt top. I have never made one of these, but experts say "a Star of Bethlehem quilt is one of the most difficult patterns to cut and sew. Hundreds of diamond patches, each having two to four bias sides, must be handled with precision.

"The technical and creative skill of American women is confirmed also by the color arrangement of the patches. Although usually composed of many different scrap fabrics, circles of delicate tone-on-tone color appear to ripple—or explode—toward the eight points of the design."[1]

Yesterday, my friend Deb told me that she had just made her first quilt for her daughter's upcoming wedding—a Star of Bethlehem. After working for months to piece it all together, she took one look at the quilt top and decided that the center-most piecing was the wrong color of green. She said, "So I cut it out and proceeded to try and piece in another center of a deeper shade of green. All my measurements were the same, but still it didn't fit."

Soon Deb realized that she had neglected to preshrink the fabric on this new centerpiece, so she soaked just that portion in hot water. Much to her relief, the star became flat and symmetrical.

This is just one example of how much quilters need a deep desire and fortitude to make such a quilt. There are

many star patterns that require less precision. However, the Star of Bethlehem is still popular and is probably the single, most-known pattern among non-quilt makers. "The number of completed Star of Bethlehem quilts in our museums is evidence of how many artisans successfully reached the end of that journey. It is for us to wonder how many quests were abandoned half-done, as stacks and stacks of diamond patches were strung together by color and neatly laid away in boxes."[2]

These abandoned quests cause me to wonder about the Wise Men. Surely there were more than three astrologers who saw that great star in the eastern sky so long ago. But maybe the others simply gave up on their journey or lost their focus and never pursued the source of that great phenomenon.

In my studies I have learned that the Magi were Gentile astrologers from Persia (now Iran). According to Larry Wood, "They were well-known in their day for their scientific knowledge and their knowledge of the heavens. The Magi who came to Jerusalem were the result of the evangelism of Daniel while he was a captive in Babylon. Daniel's wisdom was unsurpassed in astrology. The Magi accepted the prophecies of Daniel as the Word of God. They were so certain of the events in the heavens and their meaning that they set out on a journey to Jerusalem to meet the newborn King of the Jews, the Messiah of the world."[3] These Magi asked, "Where is He who has been born King of the Jews? For we have seen His star in the East, and have come to worship Him" (Matt. 2:2 NKJV).

When so many were totally unaware of the significance of the baby born in the barn, the Magi, who were believers,

brought the message that even the heavens radiated the true birth of a Savior. They used celestial splendor and divine glory to tell the world about the birth of Christ.

Are you going on a journey? One of my friends loves to remind me to "pray there before you go there." How easy it is to lose focus, to get sidetracked in minutiae, and forget why we started in the first place. Have you ever tried to do research on the Internet? First we have to search for the topic. Then we are presented with a multitude of paths to choose. We click on one, and after reading the material, we are tempted by their link page. So we click on a few of their links and are then linked to more. *This can go on for hours.* The danger is that our original research destination may have been greatly compromised by all the tempting side roads we followed.

How can we keep our focus when we can't see the entire picture? Surely those who quilt the magnificent Star of Bethlehem must long to know how all those little diamonds will look when fitted together. And yet, they won't know unless they persist and persevere to the end. This is certainly a lot like life, and it is another reason why I see my life as a quilt.

I am reminded of a favorite, yet haunting, Christmas story, "Star over Bethlehem," written by Agatha Christie. The author imagines a scene where Mary is alone with her newborn in the stable and visited there by an angel. This angel offers to show her glimpses of the future of that precious baby in her arms.

He then proceeds to show her scenes of things to come. As she watches Jesus kneeling in despair in the Garden of Gethsemane, Mary wonders why he doesn't appear to have

any friends. When the angel shows her Jesus carrying a cross up a hill to be executed, Mary is astounded that he would be grouped with criminals. In despair, she protests to the angel that surely her son would never grow up to be the pathetic man who is depicted by these scenes.

The angel responds, "What I have shown you is Truth. . . . You have seen the future. It is in your power to say if your child shall live or die."

Though pressured by the angel, Mary responds, "But since God has given him life, it is not for me to take that life away. For it may be that in my child's life there are things that I do not properly understand. . . . It may be that I have seen only *part* of a picture, not the whole. My baby's life is his own, not mine, and I have no right to dispose of it."[4]

In the story, the angel leaves in a fury, quivering with pride and rage that he failed to accomplish his purpose. He plots another time to destroy the child through temptation in the wilderness. And at this point in the story, the reader realizes that the "angel" is Lucifer, the "son of the morning" (Isa. 14:12 NKJV), who went against God and was banished from heaven.

Christie's fictional account always makes me ponder how tempted we are to interpret life with only limited information. Today my friend Peg asked me to pray for a young couple who has just given birth to a baby with Down syndrome. They have rejected the child and refuse to offer him a part in their lives. I'm sure this young couple is scared and think that they know all that the future holds. But they cannot know it until the whole picture is made complete.

None of us knows the future. We must keep plodding along (and occasionally even skipping along), one day at a time. All we have is this moment, this part of the puzzle—this piece of the patchwork. We must remember: all that looks like destruction will not necessarily destroy.

Perhaps you are in a situation where you are sorely tempted to give up. Has God clearly shown you this path? Or could it be you have become sidetracked by others, caught up by the doomsayers or the "links" that promise more and more and more.

The story of the exploratory space probe, *Pioneer 10,* launched by NASA in 1972, gives another great example of how far we can go if we don't give up. In his book *Pastoral Grit,* Craig Brian Larson discusses that event:

> According to Leon Jaroff in *Time*, the satellite's primary mission was to reach Jupiter, photograph the planet and its moons, and beam data to earth about Jupiter's magnetic field, radiation belts and atmosphere. Scientists regarded this as a bold plan, for at that time no Earth satellite had ever gone beyond Mars, and they feared the asteroid belt would destroy the satellite before it could reach its target.
>
> But *Pioneer 10* accomplished its mission and much, much more. Swinging past the giant planet in November 1973, Jupiter's immense gravity hurled *Pioneer 10* at a higher rate of speed toward the edge of the solar system. At one billion miles from the sun, *Pioneer 10* passed Saturn. At some two billion miles,

it hurtled past Uranus; Neptune at nearly three billion miles; Pluto at almost four billion miles. By 1997, twenty-five years after its launch, *Pioneer 10* was more than six billion miles from the sun.

And despite that immense distance, *Pioneer 10* continued to beam back radio signals to scientists on Earth. "Perhaps most remarkable," writes Jaroff, "those signals emanate from an 8-watt transmitter, which radiates about as much power as a bedroom night-light, and takes more than nine hours to reach Earth."

The Little Satellite That Could was not qualified to do what it did. Engineers designed *Pioneer 10* with a useful life of just three years. But it kept going and going. By simple longevity, its tiny 8-watt transmitter radio accomplished more than anyone thought possible.[5]

I believe the Christian life is, as Nietzche once said, "a long obedience in the same direction." My direction is to follow that Star of Bethlehem—the Hope of the world, the true Messiah—and to never give up. Why don't you come too?

CHAPTER TWELVE

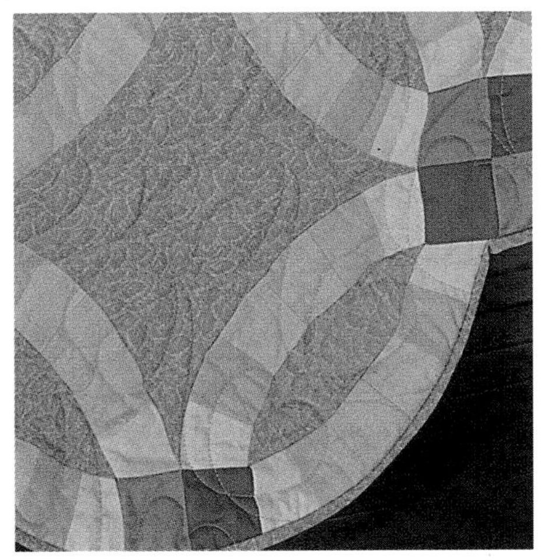

DOUBLE WEDDING RING

My husband once removed his wedding ring and put it on the table beside me. I was crushed.

He had every right to be frustrated, even angry, in the middle of our disagreement. I'm the first to admit that life with me is no picnic. I am stubborn and intense and have a way of pushing too hard. But even though I could sympathize with Mike's exasperation at the time, I still felt that taking off his ring was going a bit too far. After a few minutes Mike also thought better of his actions, and his wedding ring went back on.

Whew!

Even in the heat of the moment, we both remembered the part of our Double Wedding Ring ceremony where the minister emphasized that the circular ring is a symbol of eternal love without end: "With this ring, I thee wed . . ."

I doubt that any bride or groom on their wedding day ever dreams of a time when one of them might be sorely tempted to remove that symbol of lasting love. But sometimes, the feelings of love don't last. And it is in these times when a symbol, like a wedding ring, serves as a reminder of the covenant with one another and with God.

It is unknown when wedding rings were first worn, but it is assumed they were made of a strong metal that wouldn't break easily (for that would have been a bad omen indeed). "The ancient Romans believed that the vein in the third finger ran directly to the heart, so wearing the ring on that finger joined the couples' heart and destiny."[1]

I'll be the first to admit that when I finally entered the blissful state of matrimony at age thirty-one, I brought with me some pretty unrealistic expectations. Of course, you couldn't have convinced me of that at the time. After all, I had observed the rise and fall of marriages all around me for years. Mine would be different (in other words, "better"). Mike loved the Lord. I loved the Lord. What's not to work?

Plenty, I discovered.

First, there was self-centeredness—mine. Here's a case in point. To marry Mike, I moved eight hundred miles. I left my job and my office, but I brought my library to what was an already full house. It was one thing to resign from professional ministry; it was quite another to give up easy access to my

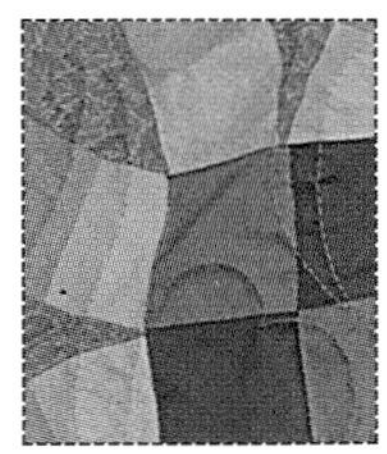

books and typewriter. At the time, I didn't think I could survive without them. So when I asked my fiancé to please convert the end of the family room into a study so I'd have somewhere to write and put my library, he did.

It never occurred to me at the time that this was a pretty outrageous request. I didn't think about whether or not Mike had money for remodeling, or that the one playroom in the house for our three small children would be drastically reduced in size (a fact that haunted me later during those long, rainy Seattle winters when the kids were "bouncing off the walls"), or that my demands were bypassing an important marital exercise called "making decisions together." My request made sense to me! After all, it was what *I needed.*

Looking back, I admit I'm extremely grateful for that study; it literally helped me survive a somewhat challenging and often amusing transition into marriage and motherhood. Interestingly enough, I have never asked for my own study in our subsequent three houses. I like to think God was working on me and helping me distinguish the difference between what I *wanted* and what I truly *needed.* (By the way, I'm writing this book in one of the kid's bedrooms. After all, that's where the family computer is.)

But selfishness is not the only threat to a marriage. There is also what some have referred to as the idea of "selective service," or living in a sort of dependent/independent relationship.

Well, I've been there too! In other words, when I wanted to be *independent,* I would be. And when I wanted to be *dependent* on Mike, then, by golly, he'd better be dependable!

But we can't selectively decide in marriage what days to show mutual love, obedience, respect, and servanthood anymore than we can in a life of following Christ.

The world says, "If it feels good, do it. And when it doesn't feel good anymore, leave." However, God says, "I have made a covenant with you, and you have made a covenant with one another. I will give you what you need to keep that covenant." Our wedding rings stand as a symbol of that promise to one another before God.

Double Wedding Ring is another very popular quilt pattern made of intertwining circles, each consisting of various fabric squares. No one knows the exact origin of the pattern, but it came into popularity in the early 1900s. At that time, the pattern appeared in newspapers, and it became a tradition for friends and family to present a Double Wedding Ring quilt to the bride as a wedding gift. Some quilt historians believe that the Double Wedding Ring pattern has been stitched more than any other quilt design. Certainly it symbolizes the hope and promise of a new beginning of committed life together.

One of the Bible passages read at our wedding ceremony also gave this promise: "They will be my people, and I will be their God. I will give them singleness of heart and action, so that they will always fear me for their own good and the good of their children after them. I will make an everlasting covenant with them: I will never stop doing good to them, . . . I will rejoice in doing them good and will assuredly plant them in this land with all my heart and soul" (Jer. 32:38–41).

Let's face it: marriage as an institution is in deep trouble. None of us wants to become yet another statistic in a marriage

that "failed." Dan Allendar and Tremper Longman, two psychologists who have spent their lives encouraging marriage partners, say that life is a battle and marriage is a part of that battle: "It is a battle that calls us to engage the enemy and push back the forces of chaos. The battle requires bold love, forgiveness, confrontation, repentance. It will involve suffering and humiliation. But the beauty of marriage is that it is God's gift of an intimate ally in the struggle."[2]

Do you see your marriage partner as an "intimate ally" or as the "enemy"? Perhaps it is time to look again at the picture of the Double Wedding Ring quilt that so clearly represents two lives intertwined together. Together, we can be intimate allies in the battles of life. Apart, we can only hope for small skirmishes won or lost, but never resolved.

My favorite daily devotional book is *My Utmost for His Highest* by Oswald Chambers. Though he actually died quite young, his wife, Biddy, had faithfully written down all his talks. That's how she was later able to put them together into a marvelous book that has sustained and guided so many who seek God's face each day. What a marvelous act of selflessness it was for Chambers' wife to daily take time to record his words by hand. She didn't know that he would die young. She wrote down his talks because she wanted to be a partner in his ministry. And God has honored her faithfulness to him in so many ways through the ministry of these devotional writings over the years.

The Chambers' biographer tells of their unique marriage: "They encouraged each other by walking individually with God and finding His grace sufficient to meet their needs. Together, their lives intertwined into a cord of shared ministry

that was stronger than either could have woven alone."[3] What a great statement for how marriages were meant to be!

Norman and Joyce Wright, a contemporary couple who have also hung in there over the long haul, offer their ten top ways to stay married happily:

1. *Share interest in your mate* to discover what has been experienced during the day and to uncover any upset feelings. This means spending time listening to and looking at each other.

2. *Show affection consistently.* Sit side by side, touch one another gently, stroke a shoulder—and not just when you want sex.

3. *Care and be kind.* Think of little things to show your love, like leaving a love note under a pillow.

4. *Show support and empathy.* Hear one another out when in disagreement and remind yourself and your mate that it's OK to feel frustrated or to not agree. Differences can make you a stronger team.

5. *Keep a sense of humor.* Balance the serious side with fun. Remind yourself of things that seemed difficult at the time but are funny now. Today's stuff could be funny tomorrow.

6. *Avoid the "takens."* Never become complacent or take your mate for granted. Think of one way you could affirm your mate each day and share that.

7. *Curb the criticism.* Think twice before you rail at your mate. One zinger can undo twenty acts of kindness.

8. *Choose hope over futility.* When you're frustrated, ready to throw in the towel, remember a time you felt that way before: How was your angst resolved? Remind yourself that a good outcome can happen again.

9. *Pray together.* Prayer opens lines to God and one another and reduces competitiveness because you're both submitted to the Lord. Pray daily, specifically and honestly, and ask God to bless your mate.

10. *Establish a vision for your marriage.* Write out what you want to accomplish as mates and the steps to get there.[4]

I still have a lot to learn about marriage. This year my parents will celebrate their golden wedding anniversary. Fifty years! They have taught me so much. My own anniversary celebration will be fifteen years! Of course, marriage is hard. Anyone who has chosen to die to self and serve another in love will confess that it's a stretch. Giving our lives for others goes against our wills and everything the world shouts at us about looking out for number one.

I have a copy of my wedding vows taped into my little prayer notebook, and I read them each day. I am intensely grateful to God, and to my husband Michael, that indeed the Double Wedding Ring is an ongoing part in the quilt of my life.

CHAPTER THIRTEEN

TRIP AROUND THE WORLD

I wasn't prepared for Hong Kong—the skyscrapers juxtaposed with the poverty, or the sea of humanity that was always in my sight wherever I went. On my first day in Hong Kong, I probably saw more people than I had seen in my cumulative twenty-five years of life thus far.

I had left Boston more than thirty hours before and had read two full books on the plane. Hoping the in-flight movie would kill at least two hours, I was disappointed to discover that since I was flying China Airlines, the movie was a kung-fu type in the Mandarin language. In hindsight, I realize that I shouldn't have been surprised, but this was

my first venture overseas outside a European country, and I was incredibly naive.

My parents were supposed to meet me as I cleared customs. I was thankful it was all arranged because I was dog tired. (Only two days before, I had returned from a month-long wilderness backpacking trip.)

But they weren't there. There were, however, hundreds of Chinese schoolchildren dressed in uniforms who ran up to me and wanted my autograph. I have no idea who they thought I was. But not wanting to disappoint them, and figuring that to them we Americans all "looked alike," I signed the name of the current pinup rage at that time—Farrah Fawcett.

That seemed to placate them for awhile, so I turned to a European-looking businessman (who was under no illusions that I was Farrah Fawcett), asked him to watch my suitcase (I told you I was naive—I still can't believe I did that!), and set off to find a genteel Southern couple with a worried look. My folks and I were soon united, my luggage miraculously retrieved, and the first of my several journeys to Asia had begun.

Before I was thirty, I had traveled around the world twice—some was business, some was pleasure. Most of the time I had been alone, which gave God some great opportunities to rescue me from quite a few near misses and wrong paths.

Trip Around the World is the name of the pattern for the second quilt I made, back in 1975. I chose primary colors of calico prints to form the pattern of squares that begin in the middle and continue around and around and around. I slept

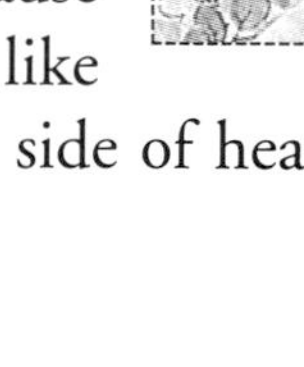

under that quilt for many years, and now it graces the sofa bed in our family room, where guests often rest from their own trips around the world.

Today it is popular to refer to our spiritual lives as a "faith journey." I like that term because I firmly believe that sanctification (becoming like Jesus Christ) will not be totally realized this side of heaven. Our whole lives are a journey:

> *Blessed are those whose strength is in you,*
> *who have set their hearts on pilgrimage. . . .*
> *They go from strength to strength. (Ps. 84:5,7)*

I'm quite certain that many of the women who first developed this patchwork design, Trip Around the World, felt like pilgrims. The Greek word for *pilgrim* is *pareipidemos,* which simply means "people who spend their lives going someplace." For those of us who have chosen to be followers of Christ, we are spending our lives going to God. We know the destination (heaven and eternity), and we also know that the only path for us is through Jesus Christ.

My friend, Maggie Rowe, once gave a powerful charge to the women of New England to encourage us on our journeys: "My dear sisters, God has no stopwatch to measure our success by our speed: how fast we go or how much we accomplish. He has no odometer to measure success by our years of service: how many miles we put on. His standard of success is simply submission to His will—that we run the race marked out for us. The race is marked, the course is set, and the flags are up. We are not

to back up, give up or let up until we see the finish line!"[1]

My daddy once said that there are basically two kinds of world travelers: those who have every little detail planned well in advance, and those who like to be spontaneous and see where each day's journey will lead. I must confess that I am most definitely of the first group. I like to plan for any contingency and be prepared.

International travel, however, has taught me that all too often I am totally at the mercy of uncontrollable factors. In the past, those have been such things as customs agents in Cairo (who inexplicably absconded with my passport for several hours), taxi drivers in Bangkok (who got caught in major traffic jams even though we left for the airport in plenty of time), small missionary planes landing on postage-stamp-size airstrips in Mexico (I had to ride in the cargo hold that time), strikes by airline workers, ice storms, overbooking, and rerouting through a totally undesirable destination.

In all those situations, there was nothing I could do. *Nothing*. How remarkable a teaching ground that position is for someone like me who desires control. Needless to say, during such times God has me where he wants me. And he never lets me proceed without first submitting to his will.

Saint Augustine once prayed, "Father, You are full of compassion. I commit and commend myself unto you, in whom I am, and live, and know. Be the Goal of my pilgrimage, and my Rest by the way. Let my soul take refuge from the crowding turmoil of worldly thoughts beneath the shadow of your wings; let my heart, this sea of restless waves, find peace in you, O God. Amen."

But our journeys are not just about destinations and fortitude—they are also about baggage. Personally, I still struggle with packing too much. I have a good excuse though—it's in my genes. While other moms were teaching their daughters how to cook, mine was showing me how to sit on overflowing suitcases and force the lock to close. In our family we took the Girl Scout motto literally: "Be prepared." I never went anywhere without a raincoat, umbrella, extra underwear, a sweater, walking shoes, makeup, curling iron, pumps, and a "little black dress" (just in case).

However, now that I'm middle-aged and my trips are usually confined to weekend speaking jaunts around my own country, I am discovering the freedom of carry-on wheelies. It's amazing how much one can cram into a small suitcase and briefcase! It doesn't matter if I'm not prepared for every situation—there are now shops on every corner.

What baggage are you still carrying around on your journey? (And I'm not talking about Samsonite here.) What is your heavy load? Think of it more as a backpack full of all your hurts, pain, unforgiveness, and shattered dreams. It sure gets harder and harder to keep walking, doesn't it? Why don't you sit at the feet of Jesus and imagine yourself emptying that backpack?

Take a moment to symbolically take out each incident, each person, each time you were hurt or inflicted hurt on someone else, and lay them at the feet of a loving Savior who has been longing to give you freedom from your baggage. Remember he is the one who says, "Come to me, all you who are weary and burdened, and I will give you rest. Take my yoke upon you and learn from me, for I am gentle and

humble in heart, and you will find rest for your souls. For my yoke is easy and my burden is light" (Matt. 11:28–30).

In *When I Got on the Highway to Heaven, I Didn't Expect Rocky Roads,* author Jeanne Zornes says, "*Rocky road* is not a flavor of nutty ice cream. It's the nitty-gritty of life. It's learning that getting where we want isn't always easy. Sometimes life's journey is rutted and rocky and rough. We're not where we want to be, and yet we don't see how things can get any better. But God knows all about our despair."[2]

What baggage are you still carrying
around on your journey?
What is your heavy load? Think of it
more as a backpack full of all your hurts,
pain, unforgiveness, and shattered dreams.
It sure gets harder and harder to keep
walking, doesn't it?
Why don't you sit at the feet of Jesus and
imagine yourself emptying that backpack?

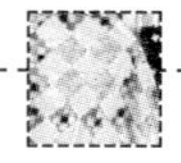

My own journey of following God has certainly taken me places I never planned or hoped to go. Often the road was narrow and difficult to maneuver. Sometimes the intersections were quite confusing, and I chose the wrong path and went down an alley from which I needed to be redirected. Much of the time I felt alone on the journey—until I was sent companions to help along the way.

I'm still moving forward, by the grace of God. And I'm thankful for every stitch as the Trip Around the World is quilted into my life's pattern.

CHAPTER FOURTEEN

JOB'S TEARS

I cried for two days.

But that was almost a week later—*after* I had to be strong for everybody else; *after* I had flown South for the funeral; *after* I had given her daughter a manicure, and sought to comfort her grieving sisters, and listened to her young widower's attempt at explanation . . .

. . . *after I had read the suicide note she left me!*

My lifelong closest friend, my touchstone between childhood, youth, and now middle age, had died violently by her own hand. The world would never be the same again.

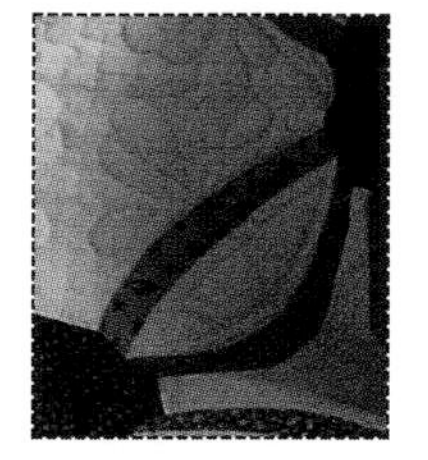

Job's Tears is a quilt pattern that was inspired by the biblical story of Job, the man who loved God but who suffered all the same. It is a story of reward and punishment, hope and despair—much like the lives of early quilters who daily faced hardships that seemed "unfair." Anne Bradstreet was a Puritan who lived in Colonial New England and wrote of her own emotional response to crises. What follows is a portion of her poem, "Some Verses upon the Burning of Our House, July 10, 1666":

And when I could no longer look,
I blest his Name that gave and took,
That layd my goods now in the dust:
Yea so it was, and so 'twas just.
It was his own: it was not mine;
Far be it that I should repine.

Anne's words epitomize Job's Tears: "when physical and emotional pain, both actual and feared, become too great, our only solace is in God who gives us life and love."[1]

It was perhaps just such an event that led the first woman to name her new quilt design Job's Tears. "Perhaps her mind was prompted by a tall grass of the same name, imported from India. The ornamental grass grows a shiny, pearl-gray seed in the shape of a teardrop. This bead, about the size of a cherry stone, is very hard and was used to make rosaries, jewelry, and other ornaments. The formed teardrop would recall Job's cry in Job 16:20: 'Mine eyes poureth out

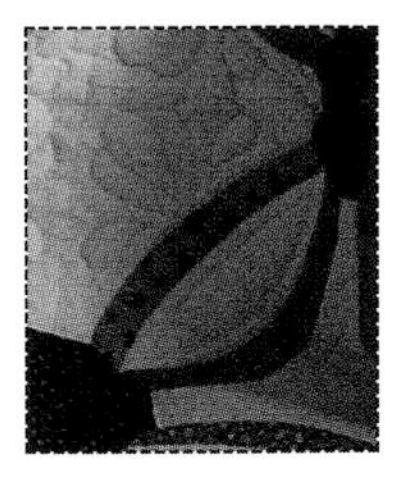

tears unto God,' and could be expressed in the oval chains of her quilt top."[2]

Author Frederick Buechner points out the importance of looking behind the tears to the reason for the tears: "Tears. You never know what may cause them. But of this you can be sure: Whenever you find tears in your eyes, especially unexpected tears, it is well to pay close attention."[3]

"Big girls do cry!" says my best friend, Maggie. In fact, Maggie even has scientific evidence to back up her claim: "Research demonstrates that women cry at least four times as often as men and that there is a clear correlation between hormones and tear production. Prolactin, the hormone that regulates the production of breast milk, is also present in tears. Since women have a much higher level of prolactin than men, researchers suggest that women are biologically better producers of tears."[4]

I knew that.

At least I know that women cry a lot—from experience. But I never thought about our tears as being a gift to offer back to God until Maggie went to the Holy Land and brought me a replica of an ancient tear cup from the Roman period. It is a tiny exquisite glass bottle with a large-lipped opening. Women in biblical times literally saved their precious tears in such intricate containers.

The use of a vessel for catching tears is first mentioned in the Bible in Psalm 56:8, where the psalmist cries in his pain to God, "Put my tears in your bottle" (NRSV). This request that God not forget the psalmist's tears is a moving image of God's depth of compassion and concern for his people.

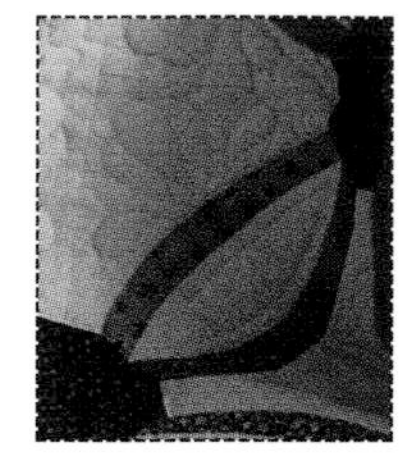

In fact, it is quite possible that the woman who washed Jesus' feet with her tears (Luke 7:37–38) was actually emptying a lifetime of precious tears to give her Savior. Some believe that Jesus' teaching had so much helped the woman that she no longer felt it necessary to save her past grief in a tear cup. Instead, she poured it all out at Jesus' feet.

The saints of old saw crying as a grace or a gift. They called it the *charism of tears.* I'm reminded of the little girl who was late getting home from school and had to answer her worried mama's question, "Why are you so late?"

"I had to help another girl who was sad," her daughter replied.

"What did you do to help her?" asked the mom.

"Oh, I just sat down and helped her cry," said the little girl, totally unaware that she had offered her friend a *charism of tears.*

We know that Job wept, and we can understand why. "My face is red with weeping, deep shadows ring my eyes" (Job 16:16). But the Bible also says that Jesus wept (John 11:35). Joni Eareckson Tada's recent book, *When God Weeps,* is perhaps one of the most helpful books I have read recently on the subject of suffering. It was meaningful because it focuses on God, who is the only one who makes sense of our suffering, and because he weeps when we weep. I believe he will one day make clear the meaning and purpose behind every tear.

Ingrid Trobisch, a widow, believes that tears are the price we pay for loving: "Crying buckets of tears is a journey. It takes us from where we were before loss to where we'll be

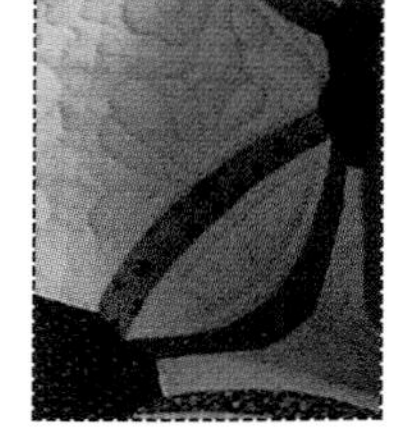

once we've adapted to the changes loss brings. . . . Allow the tears to flow. Scientists tell us they wash toxic chemicals from our bodies. Psychologists say they wash pain out of our hearts."[5]

Just last week, my friend Karen commented about how much physical and emotional energy it takes to hold back the tears. Yet, too often, we do anything to prevent the letting go of tears until finally one day the dam bursts, and we can't stop crying. Jan Dravecky, wife of baseball great Dave Dravecky, whose arm was amputated due to cancer, spent her whole life holding back the tears until she finally learned the healing catharsis of crying:

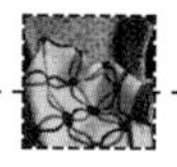

God, . . . is the only one who
makes sense of our suffering,
and . . . he weeps when we weep.
I believe he will one day make
clear the meaning and purpose
behind every tear.

I stopped and simply allowed myself to feel what I was feeling. I started to cry, and I cried for a long time. I didn't just cry; I wailed, feeling the sorrow

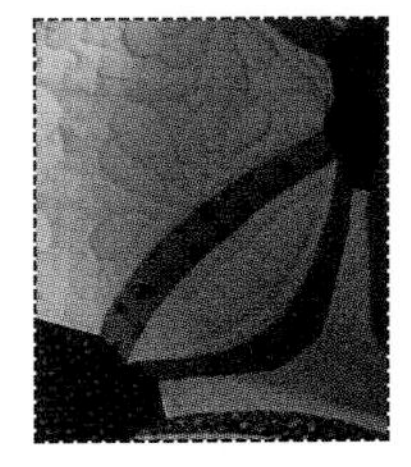

from the tips of my toes to the top of my head. I must have cried like that for at least ten minutes or more before it naturally subsided. After I was done I felt lighter; it had a cleansing effect on me. Crying felt so good that I wondered why I had avoided it for all these years. . . . I stayed with the sadness until it ran its course, and again I felt a good strong sense of relief that came from allowing the sadness to flow out with my tears.[6]

Why do you suppose women in ancient times kept their tears in a tear cup? Was it to remind them of the sadness and pain that prompted those tears? Or was it to keep as a sacrifice, an oblation to God so that he could bring beauty from those ashes? King David learned the hard way that tears could be the beginning of healing:

The sacrifices of God are a broken spirit;
a broken and contrite heart,
O God, you will not despise. (Ps. 51:17)

Later on in Psalms, we read once again that tears are a vessel of renewal:

Those who sow in tears
will reap with songs of joy.
He who goes out weeping,
carrying seeds to sow,
will return with songs of joy,
carrying sheaves with him. (Ps. 126:5–6)

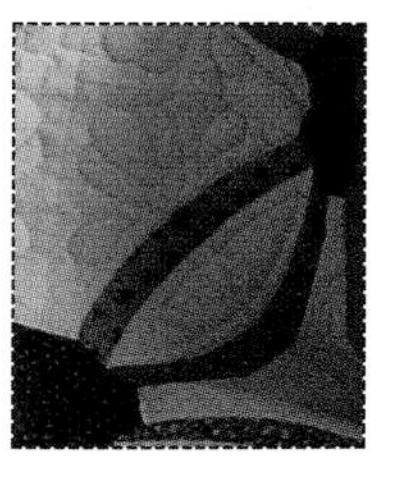

But there is a condition—we must carry "seed to sow" when we go out weeping. We must not see our tears as an end, but as a means to know God's restoration. This is what happened in the life of Job:

> *My ears had heard of you*
> *but now my eyes have seen you.*
> *The LORD blessed the latter part of Job's life*
> *more than the first. (Job 42:5, 12)*

Will that happen in your life? Will it happen in mine?

Gerald Sittser is making sure it happens in his, that his tears are the means by which he absorbs the dark threads into the patchwork of his life. A few years ago, Gerald saw the lives of his wife, mother, and four-year-old daughter snuffed out by a drunk driver. Later, he wrote about how he had to embrace rather than deny what had occurred and to search for God's grace in the midst of the horror: "I did not go through pain and come out on the other side; instead, I lived in it and found within that pain the grace to survive and eventually grow. I did not get over the loss of my loved ones; rather, I absorbed the loss into my life, like soil receives decaying matter, until it became a part of who I am. Sorrow took up permanent residence in my soul and enlarged it. . . . I picked up a paintbrush and began, with great hesitation and distress, to paint a new portrait of our lives."[7]

Gerald Sittser continues to proclaim God's grace, both in his public ministry and his family life. Would that all tears led to such restoration! Even the quilt pattern Job's Tears was eventually renamed Slave Chain during the Civil War in

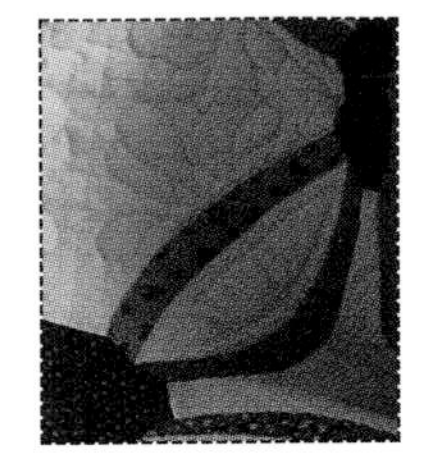

order to focus attention on that injustice. Unfortunately, sometimes, the tears are so blinding that Satan—the great enemy of all hope and restoration—wins a small battle.

Just remember: Satan will never win the war. God is the final Victor! "He will wipe every tear from their eyes. There will be no more death or mourning or crying or pain, for the old order of things has passed away" (Rev. 21:4).

The day of the funeral I went upstairs to check on my friend's young daughter. But before I did, an open door across the hall beckoned me. I probably shouldn't have done this, but I did. I walked into Cax's room and stood in front of her dresser, wondering how she felt only three days before. She had always been the smartest and most beautiful of my friends. And as a Christian counselor and pastor's wife, she had helped so many others find hope in times of crisis. As I wept over the unexplicable despair and delusion of her tortured soul, my glance caught sight of a small sheet of paper propped up on the dresser.

In her familiar handwriting I read Job's words—Job's Tears—that Cax had made her own:

I know that my Redeemer lives,
and that in the end he will stand
upon the earth.
And after my skin has been destroyed,
yet in my flesh I will see God;

I myself will see him
with my own eyes—I, and not another.
How my heart yearns within me!
(Job 19:25–27)

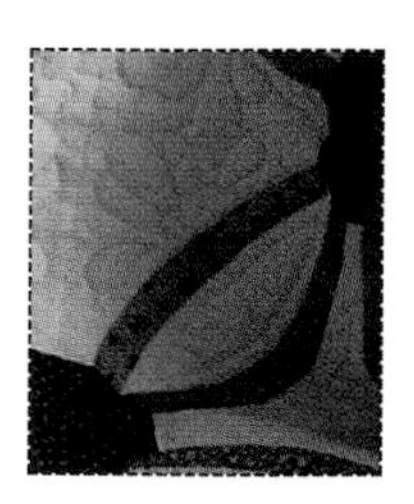

In that moment, Job's Tears were firmly woven into the quilt of my life.

This be my faith: That some day I shall see
Life's complex pattern growing plain to me;
That somewhere I shall clearly understand
The great design worked by the Master's hand;
And that somehow love's thread may reunite
Our broken lives into a fabric bright,
And in celestial arabesques restore
The ties that bind us here on earth no more.
CARRIE O'NEAL[8]

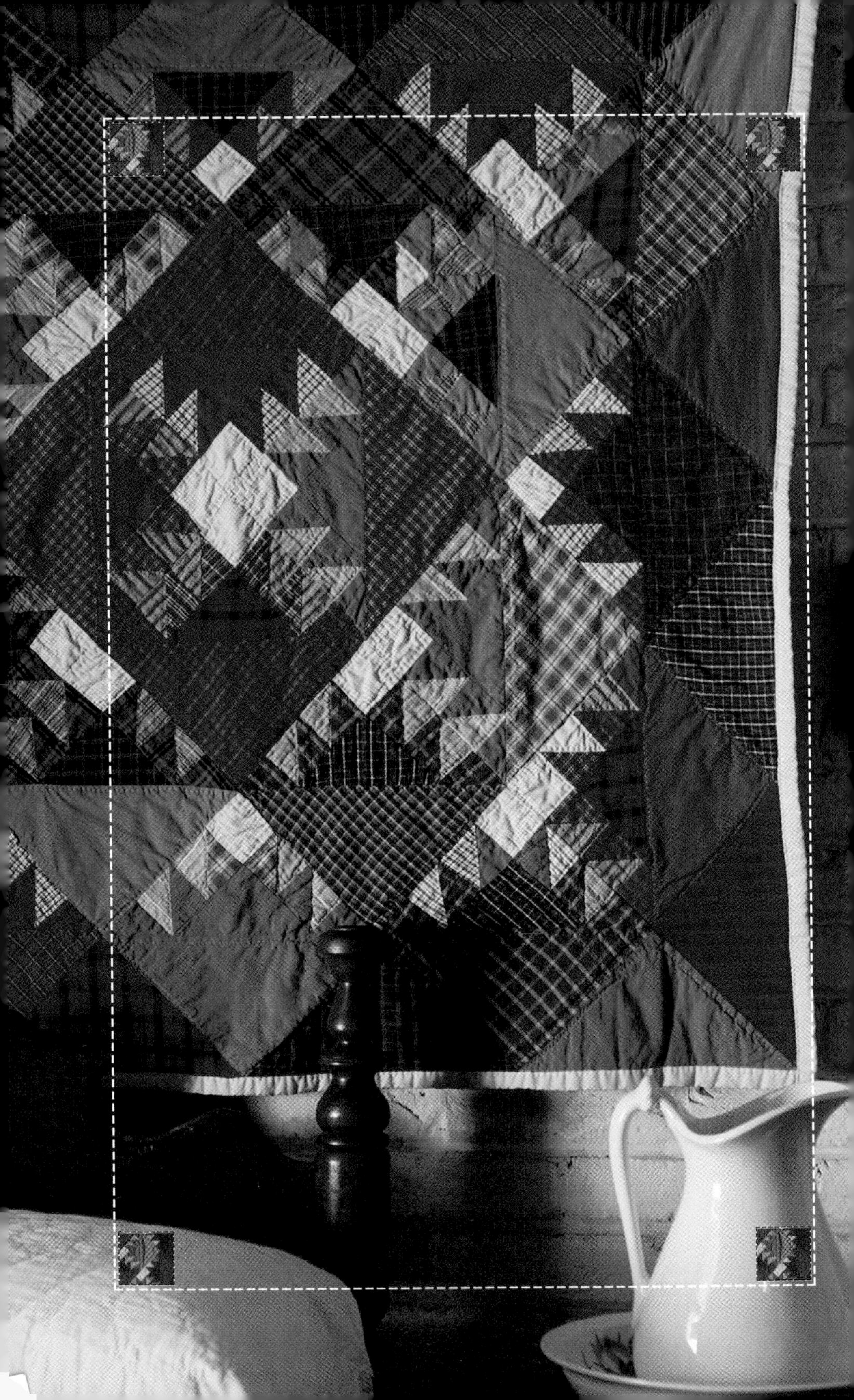

CHAPTER FIFTEEN

DELECTABLE MOUNTAINS

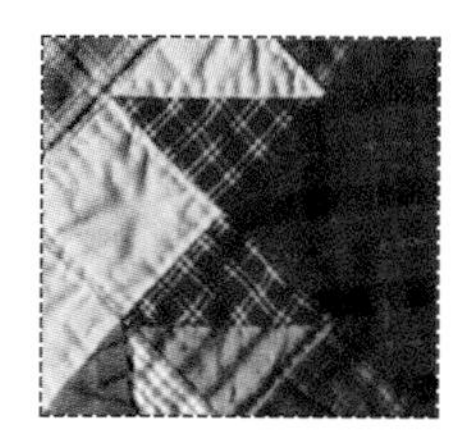

The year was 1972. The mountains were the Great Smokies. The backpackers were a ragged collection of friends from Furman University. The day was hot. The pack was heavy. The exhausted hiker was . . . me.

"How much farther to the top?" I panted to my companions. On our frequent backpacking forays, I inevitably seemed to drift into that unenviable position known as "bringing up the rear."

"Not too far, Secrest. You can make it. Keep going," one of them yelled down.

I turned with my back to the incline and gazed at the vista in front of me. Autumn in the mountains truly

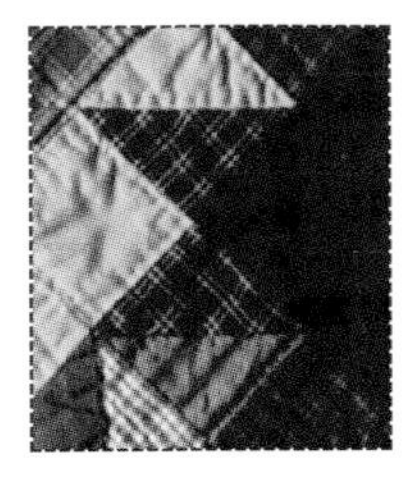

looked like God's palette of color and symmetry. How could the view higher up be any better than this!

"Look, y'all! Turn around. From here it looks like the top to me! Couldn't we just pretend we're already at the summit?"

I was desperate for a rest and quite willing to accept this partial view as reward for our day's journey.

If I had, I would have missed so much. An even grander panorama of beauty awaited us on the peak. And our celebration upon reaching the top was certainly a bonding experience.

To this day, old college friends still tease me, "Remember, Secrest, 'Looks like the top to me'!" they laugh. But, actually, it is a sobering thought to remember that I almost gave up before reaching the summit.

Christina Rossetti's nineteenth-century poem always comes to mind when I remember this mountain-climbing story:

Does the road wind uphill all the way?
Yes to the very end.
Will the journey take all day?
From morn to night, my friend.

There have been many mountains in my life since then. I have explored the Highlands of Scotland, the Swiss Alps, New England's White Mountains, Washington's Cascade Range, and the grandeur of New Zealand's Remarkables. I've ridden by donkey through Mexico's Oaxaca Mountains to remote villages where I was the first white woman they had

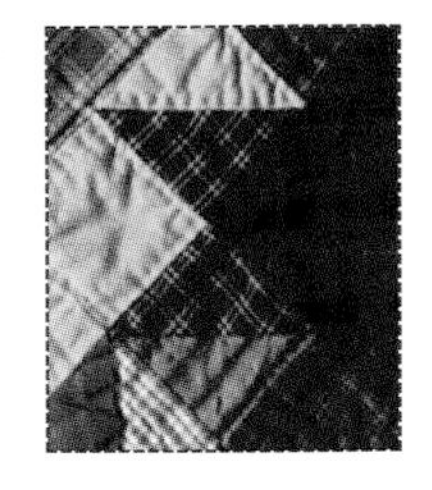

seen. And I'm soaking up inspiration right now in the heart of New York's Adirondacks.

They were all Delectable Mountains—deliciously beautiful as this quilt pattern name describes. And though the path to reach them was often difficult, I usually drew strength after having spent time in the mountains. I'm pretty sure that whatever quilter first named this pattern felt as I did. Not only that, but she was well read, since the name comes from one of my favorite books, John Bunyan's *Pilgrim's Progress.*

In this classic allegory, first published in 1678, a pilgrim named Christian is on a spiritual journey. Christian must pass through many obstacles on his way to the Celestial City: the Valley of Humiliation, the town of Vanity Fair, and also Doubting Castle.

Along the way, God sends him many companions. Early in the journey, Christian receives refreshment and encouragement in the home of Discretion, Prudence, Piety, and Charity. Before he leaves, they point out the Delectable Mountains so that he will know he is on the right path: "When morning came they took him to the top of the house and told him to look south; so he did, and he saw at a great distance a beautiful mountainous country, with woods, vineyards, fruits and flowers of all sorts, springs and fountains, wonderful to behold. . . . 'It is Immanuel's Land and it belongs to all pilgrims, as does this hill. And when you get there, you will be able to see the gate of the Celestial City.'"[1]

By the time Christian and his companion, Hopeful, actually arrive at the Delectable Mountains, they have been

through much suffering at the hands of Despair and Doubting. But it is in these mountains that they experience rest and joy, attended by shepherds named Knowledge, Experience, Watchful, and Sincere.

These shepherds (or pastors) welcome the weary pilgrims and give them nourishment: "We would like you to stay here a while so you can get acquainted with us; and more than that, so you can comfort yourselves with the good of these Delectable Mountains."[2]

What wonders await us on the summit! Yet the process is often tedious, is it not? Irish missionary to India, Amy Carmichael, encountered many obstacles in her climb as she sought to rescue innocent children from Hindu temple prostitution while at the same time suffering from years of chronic pain. It is no wonder she reflected upon a Swiss mountain guide's epitaph she had once seen—"He died climbing"—in her poem *The Last Defile*:

> *Make us Thy mountaineers;*
> *We would not linger on the lower slope,*
> *Fill us afresh with hope, O God of Hope,*
> *That undefeated we may climb the hill*
> *As seeing Him who is invisible.*
> *Let us die climbing. When this little while*
> *Lies far behind us, and the last defile*
> *Is all alight, and in that light we see*
> *Our Leader and our Lord, what will it be?*[3]

This past New Year's Eve, my twenty-one-year-old son was determined to climb the highest peak in New

England—Mount Washington in New Hampshire. At first I didn't take him all that seriously because of the frigid weather and the seemingly insurmountable odds against such a trip. But as the days drew nearer and equipment such as ice axes, crampons, ice boots, snowshoes, and the like began gathering in our mud room, I realized that Tim honestly expected to be the first person on the top of Mount Washington for the new year.

No matter how much his dad and I cajoled, warned, and finally pleaded with him to restrain from the dangerous journey in minus 80° windchill conditions, Tim's determination prevailed. On New Year's Eve, one climbing buddy drove in from Pennsylvania and another flew in from Georgia, and they headed for New Hampshire. It was totally out of my hands.

Late New Year's Day we received a phone call that the guys had summitted Mount Washington that day after digging a snow cave for their overnight stay. Tim's name is the first one in the peak's hiking registry for 1998. The boys had prayed, used their skills and common sense, taken every precaution they believed necessary, and then set out to meet their goal.

As I thanked God for protecting these three young men who truly love him, he reminded me that all my children need to climb their own mountains. I thought back to when I was in my early twenties and had learned similar hard lessons as I was taught to mountain climb and rappel in those same White Mountains of New Hampshire. I had been scared to death, but I had done it. When I felt I couldn't go any farther, God helped me to somehow go the rest of the

way. Remembering that achievement has boosted me many times since.

Now Tim has that same boost, that knowledge that God will help him reach the rest and joy of those Delectable Mountains, even if the journey to get there is potholed with obstacles. I don't think he'll ever forget it.

In another allegory, *Hinds' Feet on High Places*, by Hannah Hurnard, the crippled climber is named Much-Afraid. Later her name will be changed to Grace and Glory, but only after she has climbed the mountains. As you can imagine, her fears are in the forefront as the Shepherd urges her on: "Much-Afraid, I could do what you wish. I could carry you all the way up to the High Places myself, instead of leaving you to climb there. But if I did, you would never be able to develop hinds' feet, and become my companion and go where I go. If you will climb to the heights this once with the companions I have chosen for you, even though it may seem a very long and in some places a very difficult journey, I promise you that you will develop hinds' feet."[4]

In the Old Testament Book of Habakkuk we read: "The Lord God is my strength, and he will make my feet like hinds' feet, and he will make me to walk upon mine high places" (3:19 KJV).

As high and formidable as those literal mountain ranges I encountered in my life were, they were only a taste of the figurative mountains along my own journey. There have been challenges and trials so steep that I've been sorely tempted to turn my back and pretend that I've gone far enough—that what I can see must be all there is. But in those times of weary resignation, my Lord has come

through and given me his promise of hinds' feet on high places (Ps. 18:33).

I suspect some of those early quilters passed through some rough terrain—cold, hunger, and desolation—before they experienced their own refreshment in the Delectable Mountains. What were the first pioneer women's thoughts as their Conestoga wagons rounded the bend and they caught sight of the majestic Colorado Rockies? Nothing back East could have prepared them for the sight. I'll bet they were glad they hadn't turned back.

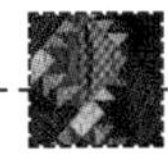

As high and formidable as those literal mountain ranges I encountered in my life were, they were only a taste of the figurative mountains along my own journey. But in those times of weary resignation, my Lord has come through and given me his promise of hinds' feet on high places.

I recently read of one Delectable Mountains quilt that has been passed down for five generations. It commemorates the survival of a nine-year-old girl, Lucinda Leonard Worth, who survived the Lost Wagon Train experience in 1853: "Over 1,500 emigrants chose to follow the suggestion of Elijah

Elliot to cut miles off the journey by heading into the southern end of the Willamette Valley, a journey taken at great risk. Because of the number of unknowns, many became lost in the rugged Cascade Mountains for up to two months. . . . The story of this particular train's experience reflects the desperation many people faced after having been as long as five months on the Trail, always seeking water and food for livestock, fresh supplies for themselves, and respite from the long journey's toll of boredom, dust, illness, and death."[5]

Though she was sickly and never expected to survive the ordeal, Lucinda lived a full life, treasuring her Delectable Mountains quilt and all it symbolized. Although she never discussed her time on the Oregon Trail, her story is just one example of how quilts were often used as silent testimonies of a seemingly insurmountable climb that was eventually conquered.

When my friend Gail MacDonald turned fifty, she and her husband, Gordon, decided to climb a mountain in Switzerland together. She is quick to point out that in such long climbs, there are more than enough challenges to make the journey both thrilling and exhausting: "Some of us are mid-lifers, and we know that the climb isn't quite the same as we thought it might be when we began. We now know what young adults can never understand: The climb is tough, exhausting, and more routine-oriented than glamorous. We know what the young do not know: You need a lot of stamina, a lot of grace, and a lot of flexibility to make it to the top."[6]

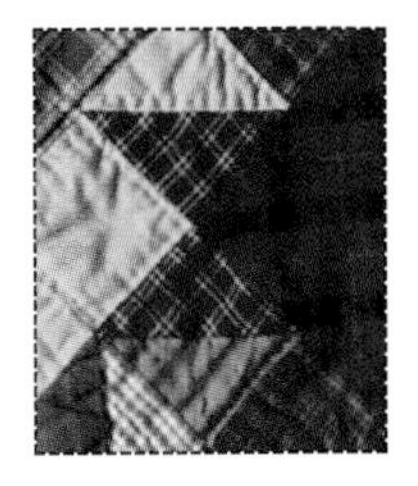

Has a mountain been plopped in the middle of your path lately? Are you tempted to give up and settle on a lower ridge because the summit seems too far away and too unknown? As God stitches the Delectable Mountains pattern into the quilt of my life, I exhort you: *Keep climbing!*

CHAPTER SIXTEEN

CRAZY QUILT

Recently Maggie, my eight-year-old daughter, started sewing her first patchwork quilt. She picked out all the fabric, and after I helped her cut it, she laid out the pieces in the pattern she desired. It is simple, but lovely—and very symmetrical. I'm pleased that she seems to have a real knack for sewing.

But as I witness the pieces coming together, I sigh. For I know that all too often life is not symmetrical or orderly. It's occasionally stressful and hectic and discouraging. And sometimes it's just plain crazy.

Today my life seems like a Crazy Quilt.

There are six baskets of laundry to be put away, the dog just threw up on the floor, the third grade room mother called to see if I would bake cookies for the class Valentine's party, my boss was just rushed to the emergency room for surgery while on a trip and I must activate the prayer chain, the speaker for an event two days away just called to say her daddy died, the bills are dangerously close to being overdue, college financial aid forms and taxes must be completed soon, I have a court date tomorrow with the Department of Mental Retardation, Maggie needs four badges sewn on her scout sash immediately, I'm a month behind delivering some Girl Scout cookies, I have a dental appointment tomorrow, my eyeglass prescription is too weak, my full-time job is taking care of hurting people and solving their problems, last month's care packages for my two kids a thousand miles away at college still haven't been sealed or mailed, the dog just got into a whole package of chewing gum, Maggie's doll was just accidentally decapitated, I have to write four more chapters for this book, our car is in the shop, and everyone wonders what I'm cooking for supper.

And that was just during a one-hour period on this Sunday afternoon—our "day of rest." Ha!

Ever had days like that? Does the Crazy Quilt seem to be a metaphor for your life? Do you feel that all your pieces are scattered and strewn far and wide without making any sense? The original patterns were meant to convey beauty and even opulence. How we have digressed!

Crazy Quilts are unlike the other patterns in this book—they are seemingly haphazard and discordant. But their popularity rose dramatically just after the 1876 Philadelphia

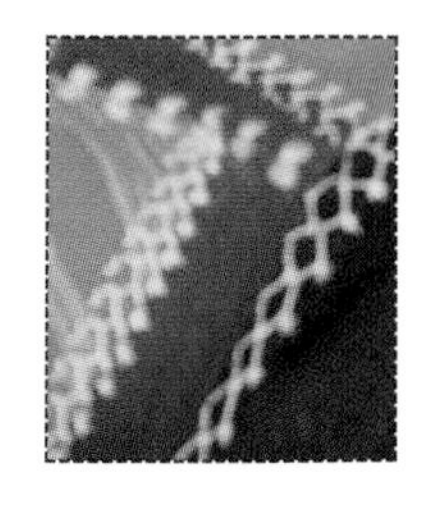

Centennial Exposition. Inspired by the Japanese pavilion, Victorian society became fascinated with Japan and its asymmetrical art. Women began showing off their needlework skills on beautiful velvets, silks, and brocades. "These quilts were more show pieces than functional and were usually smaller unquilted 'lap robes' used to decorate the parlor. They were the perfect showpieces for the lavish interior decoration of the day. To the Victorians the word *crazy* not only meant wild but also broken or 'crazed' in splinters."[1]

The one redeeming factor of the Crazy Quilt is the beautiful needlework that adorns and outlines each piece. Many of them have a fan design and even jewels woven into the elegant brocade, velvet, and silk fabrics.

By 1884, it appeared to the editor of *Dorcas Magazine* that "of all the 'crazes' which have swept over and fairly engulfed some of us, there is none which has taken a deeper hold upon the fair women of our land than this one of crazy patchwork."

It seems to me that, a little over one hundred years later, the fair women of our land are consumed in a craziness not unlike our Victorian sisters. On the outside we are younger looking, healthier, and more fashionable than women of any century. But on the inside, our lives are a crazy knot of conflicting responsibilities and duties and dreams.

What to do? The Bible says, "Be still and know that I am God" (Ps. 46:10). When was the last time you were *still*? Even Jesus Christ, whose job was to save the entire world—past, present, and future—took time each day to be still and listen: "Very early in the morning, while it was still dark,

Jesus got up, left the house and went off to a solitary place, where he prayed" (Mark 1:35).

I know I cannot face the day without a time of peace and devotion. Before the myriad of demands swirl in on me and transform me into chaos, I must sneak down into our living room, wrap myself up in an old quilt, and take time to pray, read my Bible, and share concerns of each one of my loved ones with my heavenly Father, who loves them even more than I do.

I can't go very far into my day without needing God's grace and forgiveness. I certainly identify with the prayer my friend Steve Brown shared in a letter recently:

> Dear Lord,
>
> So far today I've done all right. I haven't gossiped, lusted, lost my temper, haven't been greedy, nasty, grumpy, selfish or overindulgent. I'm very thankful for that.
>
> But in a few minutes, Lord, I'm going to get out of bed.
>
> From then on I'm probably going to need a lot of help.
>
> Amen

Crazy Quilts are not the enemy. Last spring, after I spoke on this subject in Massachusetts, Evelyn, one of the

event organizers, came up to me and gave me a tiny Crazy Quilt made by her grandmother in 1886. It is beautiful, and I treasure what it symbolizes to me. It is a reminder of what is important and how quickly life can urge us to settle for the urgent, rather than the best.

One Texas quilter, Mary White, explains that quilting is an expression of how she sees the world:

> You can't always change things. Sometimes you don't have no [sic] control over the way things go. Hail ruins the crops, or fire burns you out. And then you're just given so much to work with in a life and you have to do the best you can with what you've got. That's what piecing is. The materials [sic] is passed on to you or is all you can afford to buy . . . that's just what's given to you. Your fate. But the way you put them together is your business. You can put them in any order you like. Piecing is orderly. First you cut the pieces, then you arrange your pieces just like you want them. I build up the blocks and then put all the blocks together and arrange them, then I strip and post to hold them together . . . and finally I bind them all around and you got the whole thing made up. Finished.[2]

I want my pieces to be orderly. I don't want to be so fragmented that no beauty shines through. I still harbor regret for all those times I was driven and busy and didn't stop to smell the flowers. I need to take time to do the hard work of "embroidery"—those "extras" that make life beautiful.

My friend, Faith, often warns me: "The main thing is to keep the main thing, the main thing." Another friend, Ed, reminds me: "Don't sweat the small stuff. By the way, it's all small stuff." How often I get sidetracked. But I suspect you do too.

About five years after the Crazy Quilt hysteria began, the ladies' magazines began sending forth the decree to cease and desist. "In December 1887 *Godey's Ladies Book* stated: 'We regretted much of the time and energy spent on the most childish, and unsatisfactory of all work done with the needle—crazy patchwork.' Yet, although the periodicals of the day sternly announced the end of the crazy patchwork craze, and although styles and taste definitely changed, quilt makers did not abandon it entirely."[3]

Even quilters can fall into the trap of perfectionism and lose sight perhaps of the real reasons they began this wonderful endeavor. One quilting expert, Ami Simms, decided to poke fun at those for whom the art of quilting became more important than the process. Several years ago she created the "Worst Quilt in the World" contest. It went on for three years, and thousands of dollars were donated in prizes.

Contestants earned points for bad design, awful color combinations, and sloppy workmanship. Said Simms, "We judged using the *Three G System.* If the quilt didn't make us *Gasp, Gag* or *Guffaw,* it was out of the running."

One winner's entry was described by Ami: "This is one of the most pitiful quilts I've ever seen. All that work, and it's so ugly. I don't know what impressed the judges more, the nauseating green polyester blend fabric, or the puckered patchwork. This quilt is so homely it hurts. We love it!"

Not only were there several "Abominable Mention Awards" also given, but contest judges selected several special recognition awards:

- Knot On Your Life Award—for hand stitching an entire quilt without knotting a single thread. Not surprisingly, much of the patchwork has fallen off exposing the blanket underneath which was used instead of batting.

- Seamed Like a Good Idea at the Time Award—for intentionally stitching a quilt inside out. Not only was the wrong side of the fabric on the outside of the quilt, but unraveling seam allowances appeared there as well.

- Now We've Seen Everything Award—for binding an entire quilt in duct tape.

But this was one contest where the "losers" went away proudly with commemorative pins that said, *"Thank Goodness I Didn't Win the Worst Quilt in the World Contest!"*[4]

It's fun to laugh at ourselves. But making choices is no laughing matter, is it? When I chose to say yes to writing this book, then I of necessity had to choose to say no to many other good things that came my way this year. When Mike and I choose to write those tithe checks to the church and various mission endeavors "right off the top," we are also choosing to forego some extras that many other families deem necessities. I choose to write my parents and my college kids every week. Sure it takes time, but it's important to me that they have a tangible note from me each week in their

mailbox (I E-mail them too, but that's not the same).

What choices do you make each day?

Sue Bender, who went to live with the Amish in order to find a simpler life, says,

> Before I went to the Amish, I thought that the more choices I had, the luckier I'd be. But there is a big difference between having many choices and making a choice. Making a choice—declaring what is essential—creates a framework for a life that eliminates many choices but gives meaning to the things that remain. Satisfaction comes from giving up wishing I was somewhere else or doing something else.
>
> Then I remember the scrap pile filled with odd pieces of material of those early quilters. Nothing was wasted. Out came those glorious quilts. I have to keep reminding myself that nothing I am doing is wasted time. I may not understand or like what is happening, but I can begin to appreciate that the impasse is another marker on the way.[5]

Why is it that when we're young, we think there are lots of throwaway moments? Yet, as we grow older, we know that each moment is precious, and we cling to them. Truly, with God, *nothing is wasted.* Quilters know that instinctively.

Back in 1832, Lydia Marie Child pointed this out in *The American Frugal Housewife*: "The true economy of housekeeping is simply the art of gathering up the fragments, so that nothing be lost. I mean the fragments of *time*, as well as

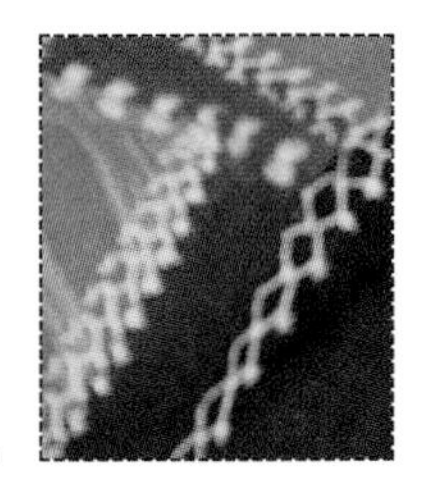

materials. Nothing should be thrown away so long as it is possible to make any use of it, however trifling that may be."[6]

I know my life has a lot of Crazy Quilt in it, but that very aspect causes me to depend on my Lord even more. I must remember the words of Isaiah 30:15: "In quietness and confidence shall be your strength" (NKJV).

Back in my Sampler days, while studying in seminary in my twenties, I had the privilege of being mentored by a woman who instilled in me the wonderful truth that nothing is wasted if offered back to God. Her name is Elisabeth Elliot. After experiencing the tragic deaths of two husbands (one speared to death by Auca Indians in Ecuador, the other by cancer), she has just now celebrated her twentieth anniversary with her third husband, Lars Gren. Truly, the pieces of her life have come together to make something beautiful for her Lord.

When I lived with Elisabeth, one of my jobs was to help in the typing of some of her manuscripts (she is the author of more than twenty-eight books). The following words from her book during those days, *Twelve Baskets of Crumbs*, are indelibly impressed upon my memory: "And although we have but fragments of a life, although we know even ourselves only in a fragmented way, eternity has been written in our hearts, and the pieces will one day be put together exactly as they were meant to go. *There is no fragmentation to God.* He sees perfectly the details as well as the destinies of our lives and orders them all in beauty and love"[7] (emphasis added).

Let us not allow ourselves to become too much like Crazy Quilts. Take time to seek quiet. Gather up all the pieces of

your life and reflect upon the divine weaving of fabric and faith. Look for parables in the patchwork of your life. Know that you can be made whole. Your life can be more beautiful than you ever imagined because God, the Quilter, loves you more than you'll ever know. He will give you quilts from heaven.

And what is life? A crazy quilt;
Sorrow and joy, and grace and guilt,
With here and there a square of blue
For some old happiness we knew;
And so the hand of time will take
The fragments of our lives and make,
Out of life's remnants, as they fall,
A thing of beauty, after all.

DOUGLAS MALLOCH[8]

ENDNOTES

Chapter One

1. Dennis Duke and Deborah Harding, *America's Glorious Quilts*, Beaux Arts Edition (China: Hugh Lauter Levin Associates, Inc., 1987), 15.
2. Marlene Parkin, "Quilts—Masterpieces of the Heart and Windows into Women's History," *Americana*, 22, July/August 1993.
3. Ruth Finley, *Old Patchwork Quilts and the Women Who Made Them* (Charlie T. Branford, 1971).
4. Carleton L. Safford and Robert Bishop, *America's Quilts and Coverlet* (New York: Weavervane Books, 1974), 88.
5. Jeanne Zornes, "Remnants," *Decision Magazine*, March 1990, back cover.
6. T. Davis Bunn, *The Quilt* (Minneapolis, Minn.: Bethany House, 1993), 110.
7. Interview of The Material Girls, Bakersfield, Calif. newspaper.
8. Alice Kalso, "Life Stories Told in Stitches," *Virtue Magazine*, March/April 1991, 46.

Chapter Two

1. Christina Rossetti, "A Better Resurrection," *Eerdman's Book of Christian Poetry* (Grand Rapids, Mich.: William B. Eerdman's, 1981), 62.
2. Max Lucado, *A Gentle Thunder* (Dallas, Tex.: Word, 1995), 145.
3. T. Davis Bunn, *The Quilt*, 46.

4. Ibid., 95.
5. Ibid., 109.

CHAPTER THREE

1. Roderick Kiracofe, *Cloth and Comfort* (New York: Clarkson/Potter Publishers, 1994), 26.
2. Linda Otto Lipsett, *Remember Me: Women and Their Friendship Quilts* (San Francisco: Quilt Digest Press, 1985), 16.
3. Ibid.
4. Ibid., 24.
5. Jerry and Mary White, *Friends and Friendship* (Colorado Springs, Colo.: NavPress, 1984).
6. "TCW Survey Results," *Today's Christian Woman*, September/October 1995, 107.
7. Pat Ferraro, *Hearts and Hands: The Influence of Women and Quilts on American Society* (San Francisco: Quilt Digest Press, 1987), 52.
8. Melody Carlson, "The Crazy Quilt," quoted by Alice Gray in *More Stories for the Heart* (Sisters, Oreg.: Multnomah, 1997), 227.

CHAPTER FOUR

1. From a lenten calendar.
2. "Sunshine and Shadow," Stone Ginger Cards, (http://www.stoneginger.com).
3. Sue Bender, *Plain and Simple* (New York: HarperCollins, 1989), 4.

Chapter Five

1. Judy Mathieson, *Mariner's Compass Quilts—New Directions* (Lafayette, Calif.: C and T Publishing, 1995), 6.
2. Ibid., 10.
3. Madame Jeanne Guyon, *Experiencing the Depths of Jesus Christ* (Augusta, Maine: Christian Books, 1981), 114–115.
4. Thomas Merton, *Thoughts in Solitude* (Noonday Press, 1987), 83.

Chapter Six

1. David L. Veal, *Saints Galore*, (Cincinnati, Ohio: Forward Movement Publication, 1972), 133.

Chapter Seven

1. Susan C. Druding, "Antique Quilt Pattern History," (quilting.guide@miningco.com), 1.
2. *Where Love Resides,* compiled by That Patchwork Place, Inc. (Bothell, Wash., 1996), 13.
3. Lucinda Secrest McDowell, *Amazed by Grace* (Nashville, Tenn.: Broadman and Holman, 1996). Check your local bookstore, the publisher, or order directly from "Encouraging Words," Box 290707, Wethersfield, CT, 06129, for $11.00 postpaid.
4. Ingrid Trobisch, *Keeper of the Springs* (Sisters, Oreg.: Multnomah, 1997), 20.
5. Thomas Kinkade, *Simpler Times* (Eugene, Oreg.: Harvest House, 1996), 5.

CHAPTER EIGHT

1. Carrie A. Hall and Rose G. Kretsinger, *The Romance of the Patchwork Quilt in America* (New York: Bonanza Books, 1935).
2. Linda Riley, letter to author, November 1996. Reprint can be ordered from Called Together Ministries, 20820 Avis Ave., Torrance, CA, 90503.
3. Ibid.
4. Mack Thomas, *Through the Eyes of Jesus* (Sisters, Oreg.: Questar, 1995), 62.

CHAPTER NINE

1. Carter Houck, *The Quilt Encyclopedia* (New York: Harry N. Abrams, 1991), 164.
2. Ferraro, *Hearts and Hands*, 58.
3. Louise McCormick Gibney, "I Always Like a Challenge: A Visit with Jinny Beyer," *Traditional Quilts*, Fall 1996, 2.
4. Lucinda Secrest McDowell, *Women's Spiritual Passages: Celebrating Faith after 40* (Wheaton, Ill.: Harold Shaw, 1996). Check your local bookstore, the publisher, or order directly from "Encouraging Words," Box 290707, Wethersfield, CT, 06129, for $10.00 postpaid.
5. http://monticello.avenue.gen.va.us/arts/CAQG/history.html.
6. Louis Evans Jr., *Covenant to Care* (Wheaton, Ill.: Victor Books, 1982), 20–21.

7. Anna Quindlan, "Dear Friends," *Northeast Magazine*, 2 March 1997, 5.
8. Ibid., 15.

Chapter Ten

1. Quoted in Jean Bethke Elshtain, "Idiots, Imbeciles, Cretins," *Books and Culture*, January/February 1998, 18.
2. Quoted in Cheri Fuller and Louise Tucker Jones, *Extraordinary Kids* (Colorado Springs, Colo.: Focus on the Family, 1997), 22–23.
3. Quoted in Nancy Carmichael, "Simply Faithful, Simply Joni," *Virtue*, July/August 1993, 30.
4. V. Raymond Edman, from *Christianity Today.*
5. From a conversation with Elisabeth Elliot, Asheville, N.C., fall 1986.
6. Quoted in Elisabeth Elliot, *Keep a Quiet Heart* (Ann Arbor, Mich.: Servant, 1995), 29–30.

Chapter Eleven

1. Suzzy Chalfant Payne and Susan Aylsworth Murwin, *Creative American Quilting Inspired by the Bible* (Old Tappan, N.J.: Fleming H. Revell, 1983), 81.
2. Ibid.
3. Larry Wood, "The Christmas Story," (http:///ddi.digital.net, 1998), 9.
4. Agatha Christie Mallowan, "Star over Bethlehem," in *Miracle of Christmas* (Wheaton, Ill.: Harold Shaw, 1997), 14.

5. Craig Brian Larson, *Pastoral Grit: The Strength to Stand and Stay* (Minneapolis, Minn.: Baker Book House, 1997).

CHAPTER TWELVE

1. Melanie Ganson, "Wedding Traditions," 1995 (http://www2.rpa.net/jbretz/wed-traditions.html), quoting from *A Natural History of Love* by Diane Ackerman.
2. Dan Allender and Tremper Longman III, *Intimate Allies* (Colorado Springs, Colo.: NavPress, 1996), 107, 113.
3. David McCasland, *Oswald Chambers: Abandoned to God* (Grand Rapids, Mich.: Discovery House, 1993), 238.
4. Norman and Joyce Wright, "10 Top Ways to Stay Married Happily," *Today's Christian Woman*, Spring 1996.

CHAPTER THIRTEEN

1. Maggie Wallem Rowe, "A Challenge to New England," *Woman to Woman Newsletter*, Vision New England, Burlington, Mass., November/December 1996, 3.
2. Jeanne Zornes, *When I Got on the Highway to Heaven . . . I Didn't Expect Rocky Roads* (Wheaton, Ill.: Harold Shaw, 1998), 16.

CHAPTER FOURTEEN

1. Payne and Murwin, *Creative American Quilting*, 68.
2. Ibid.

3. Quoted by Trobish, *Keeper of the Springs*, 67.
4. Maggie Wallem Rowe, "Big Girls Do Cry," in McDowell, *Women's Spiritual Passages*, 178–179.
5. Trobisch, *Keeper of the Springs*, 67.
6. Jan Dravecky, *A Joy I'd Never Known* (Grand Rapids, Mich.: Zondervan, 1996), 171.
7. Gerald Sittser, *A Grace Disguised: How the Soul Grows through Loss* (Grand Rapids, Mich.: Zondervan, 1997).
8. Quoted in Hall and Kretsinger, *Patchwork Quilt*, 131.

CHAPTER FIFTEEN

1. John Bunyan, *The New Pilgrim's Progress* (Grand Rapids, Mich.: Discovery House, 1989), 70.
2. Ibid., 144.
3. Amy Carmichael, *Toward Jerusalem* (Ft. Washington, Pa.: Christian Literature Crusade, 1936), 99.
4. Hannah Hurnard, *Hinds' Feet on High Places* (Wheaton, Ill.: Tyndale Publishers, 1975), 62–63.
5. Mary Bywater Cross, *Treasures in the Trunk* (Nashville, Tenn.: Rutledge Hill, 1993), 153.
6. Gail MacDonald, *A Step Farther and Higher* (Sisters, Oreg.: Questar, 1993), 261.

CHAPTER SIXTEEN

1. Anne Johnson, "Our Quilting History: Victorian Crazy Quilts," *Womenfolk*, 1998 (http://www.womenfolk.com/ grandmothers/crazyqu.htm), 1.

2. Patricia Cooper and Norma Bradley Buferd, *The Quilters: Women and Domestic Art* (Garden City, N.Y.: Doubleday, 1977), 20.
3. Roderick Kiracofe, *The American Quilt* (New York: Clarkson/ Potter Publishers, 1993), 149.
4. Ami Simms, "'Totally Pathetic' Describes Winning Quilt" (http://www.quilt.com/artists/worstquilt97), 1996.
5. Bender, *Plain and Simple* (New York: HarperCollins, 1989), 141, 147.
6. Kiracofe, *Cloth and Comfort*, 52.
7. Elisabeth Elliot, *Twelve Baskets of Crumbs* (Chappaqua, N.Y.: Christian Harold House, 1976), 69.
8. Hall and Kretsinger, *Patchwork Quilt*, 163.

ABOUT THE AUTHOR

Lucinda Secrest McDowell is a conference speaker and writer currently living in New England. She is the author of *Amazed by Grace* and *Women's Spiritual Passages* and a contributing author to *Mothers Have Angel Wings, God's Abundance, The Strength of a Woman, Stepping Out,* and *Shaped by God's Love.* She has also written for more than fifty different magazines.

Cindy holds degrees from Gordon-Conwell Theological Seminary and Furman University and also did graduate work at the Wheaton College School of Communication. She has worked as a journalist, radio broadcaster, communications specialist, and missions director. She currently serves as Director of Women's Ministries for a congregational church that was "gathered" in 1635.

Cindy enjoys quilts, books, pansies, teapots, but most of all her family. She is married to Reverend Michael McDowell, and they are grateful parents of four children: Justin, Timothy, Fiona, and Margaret Sarah.

She would love to hear from you. Please write to:

"Encouraging Words!"
P. O. Box 290707
Wethersfield, CT 06129
encouragingwords@snet.net

SPECIAL THANKS

For the use of their quilts in the photographs, we gratefully thank:

- Lucinda Secrest McDowell of Wethersfield, Connecticut, for the "Friendship" quilt made in 1976 as a wedding gift to her sister, Susan Secrest Waters of Thomasville, Georgia.
- Sehoy L. Welshofer of Hendersonville, Tennessee, for "Sampler," "Log Cabin," "Windmill," "God's Eye," "Sunbonnet Sue," "Sunshine and Shadows," and "Trip Around the World."
- Sehoy L. Welshofer and Joanne Parisi of West Springfield, Massachusetts, for "Cleopatra's Ring," used on the cover.
- Irene Andrews of Nashville, Tennessee, for "Double Wedding Ring," "Mariner's Compass," "Grandmother's Flower Garden," and "Crazy Quilt."
- Suzzy Chalcant Payne of Fairport, New York and Susan Aylsworth Murwin of Doylestown, Pennsyvania, for "Job's Tears."
- Jenny Moss of Hendersonville, Tennessee, for "Broken Dishes."
- Ruby Anna Dickens of Hendersonville, Tennessee, for "Star of Bethlehem."
- Carolyn Anderson of Nashville, Tennessee, for "Delectable Mountains."

For the use of their homes and property for the photo locations, we gratefully thank:

- Larry and Elizabeth Papel of Nashville, Tennessee, for the use of the Harding-Mitchell-Drumright-Papel Cottage in Beersheba Springs, Tennessee.
- Norman and Theresa Carl of Nashville, Tennessee, for the use of Peach Blossom Cottage in Beersheba Springs, Tennessee.